In Celebration!
Rena Blumberg

Honey Girl, I don't know where you came from.
You're just so headstrong!

—*Ezra Z. Shapiro, to his daughter, Rena*

Headstrong

A Story of Conquests & Celebrations...

Living Through Chemotherapy

RENA BLUMBERG

Crown Publishers, Inc.   New York

Grateful acknowledgment is given to the following for permission to use the photographs which appear after page 18, "My Roots & Records": Joseph Darwal; Peter Frye; Reuven Rosenfelder; Carol Geddes; Harlan E. Sherman; Jonathan Lewis; Ralph Norman; Lynn S. Rebman; Sharon Dennis; IWY/ Cleveland Foundation—Ricardo Barrett, photographer; Bonita Sparrow, Southern Baptist Radio-TV Commission; Diane Hires; Herb Ascherman; the *Cleveland Press*: Timothy Culek, photographer; Lucinda Hall Baker.

Thanks also is extended to Ms. Betty Friedan and Ms. Jane Fonda for permission to use photographs of them, which appear in this book.

Finally, thanks is also given to the Hospice Council for Northern Ohio for permission to use information regarding the Council and to list the National Hospice Organization as a reference.

Copyright © 1982 by Rena Blumberg

Published by Crown Publishers, Inc., One Park Avenue, New York, New York 10016, and published simultaneously in Canada by General Publishing Company Limited

Manufactured in the United States of America

Library of Congress Cataloging in Publication Data

Blumberg, Rena.
    Headstrong

    1. Breast—Cancer—Patients—United States—Biography. 2. Breast—Cancer—Chemotherapy. 3. Blumberg, Rena. I. Title.
RC280.B8B58 1982 362.1'9699449'00924 [B]
                                        82-9770
                                        AACR2

                    ISBN: 0-517-547236
        10 9 8 7 6 5 4 3 2 1
                    First Edition

For Michael

who has brought laughter, balance and glorious living into my life

for Cathy

who campaigned for me

for David

who escorted me

for Stuart

who costarred with me, who keeps me young

and

for Pamela Thomas and Lucinda Hall Baker

my living literary network who edited the message of my life with tenacity and delicacy

CONTENTS

Photographs follow page 18.

PREFACE

One out of every thirteen women now alive in the United States will develop breast cancer at some time in their lives.

How often I had heard and read this statistic. Sometimes, if I heard this statement at a meeting or luncheon, I would look down the aisle or around the table and feel sad that someone near me in the room might soon have cancer, or might be harboring the dread disease and not even know it yet. No one expects to be number thirteen. Like any ugly statistic, the magic number always applies to someone else. Never to you or me.

But one day it *was* me.

Cancer was discovered in my left breast, and I had to face the trauma of a mastectomy and the unbelievable pain of two years of aggressive adjuvant chemotherapy. For four years, from the discovery of the first cancer in 1975 until I finished chemotherapy in the late summer of 1979, I fought this disease with all the personal strength I could bring to bear. Throughout my fight, I continued to live a full, joyous and complete life. It often took an incredible force of will on my part just to get up in the morning, let alone continue with life. But continue I did.

Today, it has been five years since I had my mastectomy. This is considered the first bench mark for optimism for the possibility of a normal life-span. (Medically, ten years are now required for clinical pronouncement of cure.) But I feel *well,* my doctors confirm this and my fears are behind me.

During my illness, many people were amazed and puzzled by my energetic immersion in celebrating each day. They would ask, How do you do it? How do you find the energy? How do you keep from quitting chemo? How do you deal with your family? How do you continue to work? Sometimes they asked for themselves, sometimes for a close friend or relative. They wanted details, minutiae. They wanted to know how I dealt with the physical problems of surgery and therapy, the emotional problems of sex and relating to my family, and the everyday problems of life—my work, my friendships, my activities.

After many hours of personal conversations and public lectures, I have decided to write about my experiences and share with others the discoveries I have made. Very early on in the writing of this book, I decided to entitle it *Headstrong*. One definition of "headstrong" is "an inclination to have one's own way." Many people might say this is not necessarily a very acceptable attitude. In still other ways, the word "headstrong" has the even more negative connotation of extreme willfulness and sometimes obstinacy.

But here, without changing the basic strength of that word, I mean "headstrong" in a very positive sense. For me, "having my own way" meant I was going to *survive*. To live—and live fully. This took willfulness, to be sure. And at certain moments, particularly during chemo, yes, it took downright obstinacy. But more than any other attitude, I feel this "headstrong" approach to coping with cancer was the quality that allowed me to survive and to get on with the business of living and living joyously.

So here is my story—my headstrong story. And here, too, are those people, qualities, attitudes and support systems, both large and small, that combined to give me strength. It is my belief that we all have the resources at hand to make us headstrong, to give us the strength to survive serious illness. The problem is to identify them, and then tap them. It is my hope that this book will help you take full advantage of your own resources and to emerge, as I have, with great hope for tomorrow.

The Beatles wrote a line that rings through my mind every day: "I survive with a little help from my friends." This is so very true for me, and I want to publicly proclaim my deep gratitude to those who helped me before, during and after the battle. With love, I thank:

My Immediate Family:

in Israel, Sylvia Shapiro
in New York, Dan, Ellen, Jon, Andrew and
    Peter Shapiro
in Cleveland, Helen, Manny and Paul Shapiro,
    Divy Lewin
in Kansas City, Mark Blumberg

My Extended Family-of-Choice:

Marilyn Blaushild, Judy and Harlan Sherman
Stuart Sherman, Nina and Norman Wain
Marilyn Yarus
The Shabbos Group, the Lag B'Omer Bunch
The Succah Builders—Bob Frankel, artistic director

My Sisters in Other Cities:

Addrianne Sherman in London
Eleanor Brenner in New York
Marcia Epstein in Winston-Salem

My Personal Support Group:

Agnes Peoples
Armand Cosenza, Tom Stazzone
Ida Lee, Al Nola, Alvin Amster

My Encouragers:

Ralph and Terry Kovel, Robert and Joanne Lewis
Nancy Hexter, Joy Jacobs, Lois Katovsky
Georgene Kravitz and Dorma Weiner
Elaine Hadden, Carol Lucas and Rose Rosenberg
I. M. Greenberg
WDOK-FM/WWWE-AM, The Gannett Broadcast
    Group
Peter Irmiter, an exceptional general manager

My Physicians and Partners:

Dr. Julian Kassen, Dr. George Goler
Dr. Richard Bornstein, Dr. Dan Butler
Dr. Mark Levine, Dr. Robert Katz
Dr. Avrum Froimsom
In an aura of lavender, Dr. Irene Hazelton

The Post Mastectomy, Rehabilitation and Oncology Team
    at Mount Sinai Medical Center:

Shirley Einbund, Sherrie Reynolds, Phyllis Hall,
    Virginia Stewart, Mary Spagnola

Those Who Help Me Feel Like a Swan:

Caritina Braun, Joey Mancuso, Rose, Gladys,
    Clara (MJ) Susan, Angie

My Networking Links at WomenSpace, Cleveland Women
    Working, and The Playhouse Square Foundation

The Neighborhood Walking Group, Brenda Goldberg,
    organizer

The Shaker Heights Public Library, Bertram Woods Branch:

Dorothy Schaffner, research associate

Those who have celebrated with me, but who are no longer here:

My Father, Ezra Z. Shapiro
My Friend, David L. Blaushild
My Guide, Dora R. Sukenik
My Surgeon, Dr. Sidney H. Sachs

Part One

Conquests: Cancer and Chemotherapy

Now I'm glad I've lived long enough to do some of the things I used to admire. Lately I only admire people who do what they have to do.

Sunshine Days and Foggy Nights
—James Kavanaugh

- 1 -

I love to celebrate!

Any excuse will do. The beginning of a new season, the first Monday in May, the forty-third birthday of a friend, anniversaries, religious holidays, the culmination of an important goal. Party-giving is the perfect creative outlet for my Perle Mesta energies, so I entertain often.

I also can't resist challenges. I embrace them with an eagerness that sometimes astonishes those around me. (I have to admit, my husband and friends say it sometimes exhausts them, too.) And parties, particularly, present a very special sort of challenge.

In December 1980, Cleveland Women Working, one of the first organized groups of women office workers in the country, asked me to open my home and help them arrange a party celebrating the premiere of the movie *Nine to Five,* in Cleveland. Jane Fonda, one of the stars of the movie, volunteered to attend the premiere—as well as the party—to help raise money for CWW.

Organizing a benefit celebration in two weeks and making it an event to remember was an ultimate challenge for me. I knew this would be a special occasion for those women, many of whom had been interviewed during the preparation of the movie and whose lives served as prototypes for the characters. So, lives were very much a part of this movie, so, swinging into action, I mobilized my troops.

We decided to stage an elegant soup and sandwich fest, and turn my home into a gigantic soup kitchen. I enlisted volunteers from all segments of my life, and many talented people made contributions. Friends brewed huge pots of mushroom-barley soup. Forty women from Cleveland Women Working prepared forty sandwiches each. A good friend, who raises orchids for a hobby, donated orchids from his own greenhouses for the centerpieces. A wonderful baker I had discovered a few years before made huge cakes that resembled typewriters, complete with jelly-roll rollers. A local cheese store proprietor created the image of a clock on a wheel of Brie, using almonds to point to nine and five.

We wanted to include as many CWW supporters as possible, but we were overwhelmed by the response to our invitation. I found I had to ask my next-door neighbor to open her house to accommodate the overflow. We called our team of volunteers and asked them to duplicate their efforts. The result? Two parties in houses side by side, each carbon copies right down to the typewriter cakes, orchid centerpieces and nine-to-five clocks made from wheels of Brie.

The night of the party arrived and, with the sold-out crowd of guests, so did the first big snowfall of the winter. The weather delayed Jane's arrival, but the excitement and anticipation kept the guests patient and good-tempered.

Finally, Jane Fonda arrived, wearing a red plaid silk blouse, a black quilted Chinese jacket and black slacks. What I noticed most about her appearance was how healthy she looked—lean, firm and tanned. Even her red-brown hair was chamomile fresh and glowing.

I had entertained Jane once before in my home, but I was excited to be welcoming her in my entry hall surrounded by friends, family, co-workers and volunteers. They were as eager to see her as I was; they could hardly wait to talk to one of the women who helped make their fantasies come alive on the screen.

And talk to her they did. Each guest had a chance to speak

to Jane personally, from the buxom blonde woman who inspired the Dolly Parton role in the movie to the man who won Cleveland Women Working's first annual "Pettiest Office Procedure" award for making his secretary slice carrot sticks for his diet lunch. She didn't awe us. The knowledge of her celebrity status was bound to create barriers in some minds, but she knocked those down with her incredible naturalness, warmth and sincerity.

After each person had spoken to Jane individually, she stood on a coffee table in front of the fireplace to address the crowd. Just as she began to speak, all the lights in the house blew out, except the two over the coffee table. I couldn't believe it! All the electric coffee makers, plugged in at once, had overloaded the system, yet the lights that remained on seemed to spotlight Jane as she spoke. One guest whispered to me, "How clever you were, Rena, to arrange this lighting to heighten the effect of Jane's presence." While I gave silent thanks for that small miracle, three of us found candles in a drawer and distributed them among the guests. Unintentionally, we created a very dramatic atmosphere.

Fortunately, Chester, a Runyonesque policeman, who was helping us by directing traffic and parking cars, located the blown fuse and saved the day. The lights came back on just as Jane finished her speech. (Another little touch of drama!) We then whisked her next door for phase two of the double-barreled benefit.

After Jane left for the theater, we volunteers kicked off our shoes, removed our party clothes and began to clean up. Imagine our surprise when a few hours later Jane returned to our scene of organized chaos. I certainly never expected her to come back to the house after the premiere because I knew she was anxious to return to California to help take care of her ailing father.

She had come to the house to spend a few relaxing minutes talking informally to us before she had to leave for the airport. She settled herself on the sofa and fed a bottle to the infant daughter of her friend, the chairperson of Cleveland Women Working, while we all chatted.

She told us about her trip to Israel with her children, her reactions to seeing the Western Wall and the Yad V'Shem, the Holocaust Memorial in Jerusalem. We talked about the Hadassah Hospital where she had been taken to have her broken leg set and where she happened to be greeted by my mother, who heads the Hadassah Council of Israel. I liked the fact that my life and hers were linked in this particular way.

Her conversation with all of us touched on some of the concerns that all women share. We discussed career opportunities and the need for equal pay for equal work. We also talked about the need to continue family traditions while recognizing and developing new family patterns. This totally unplanned chat between Hollywood star and committed volunteers was the highlight for many of us of an incredibly rewarding day.

The reason I describe this party in such detail is because it emphasizes certain patterns I have tried to incorporate into my life. The party had a purpose, to raise money for a valuable organization. The planning and the execution utilized the talents of men and women volunteers working together with a spirit of cooperation so that not the smallest detail was ignored. At this party my husband, son and family-of-choice (a small group of friends representing all ages and both sexes who are very close to and supportive of my biological family) added their strengths and support, helping to ensure the party's success. And, finally, this party, held in my home, opened my family's private place to the community for a cause I believe in deeply.

Purpose, imagination, laughter and sharing with friends and family created the magic to make a grand evening. This party symbolized for me a workable philosophy for life. The components that went into making the benefit for Cleveland Women Working such a success are the qualities that enabled me to survive when, not too long before this party, some of my most basic life patterns cracked.

6

– 2 –

Friday night, October 30, 1962, was the first time the lovely pattern of my life cracked. Until then, life had treated me very well. I had been brought up in a very warm, very secure, upper middle-class home in Cleveland, Ohio. My father was a lawyer and had his own law firm. He was active in community affairs, serving at one point as assistant mayor, and was the founder of the American Jewish League for Israel. My mother, like my father, was an inveterate volunteer. These were caring people, of their family and their community.

I had a normal happy childhood, which I shared with my brother, who was four years younger. Whatever was expected, I did. I was graduated from Cleveland Heights High School and went happily on to Brandeis University. While there, I met the handsomest man in the world, or so I thought at the time. We fell in love, later married, had two children, Cathy and David, and settled into a life that I thought would go on forever.

But on the eve of my twenty-eighth birthday, it all came apart. On that evening, my husband and I had just returned from a Sabbath dinner at my parents' apartment. We were in the kitchen when my husband calmly told me he wanted a divorce. He said he no longer wanted to be married to me. Just like that. No scene, no huge argument. Just a simple announcement.

In fact, our seven-year marriage had a storybook facade, but I was aware of trouble throughout. Like many women of the fifties, I never considered divorce as a way of solving my own unhappiness; I tried harder and thought it my duty to make the marriage work. So his calm, cold request came as a terrific blow to me, and his departure was a shock.

I was hurt, embarrassed and frightened. I worried about how to tell my parents and my friends, but most of all, I worried about how I would deal with my children alone.

My quick conclusion was to throw myself into parenting with a vengeance. I bought the children guinea pigs and hamsters on which to lavish their affection. I made sure their days were crammed with lessons: Hebrew, Dalcroze eurythmics, piano, guitar, flute and art. Name a discipline and I made sure they were well tutored in it. I got to the point where I was spending three hours a day behind the wheel of my car chauffeuring my children to some activity or other.

Because divorce was something only "bad" women did and because it wasn't socially acceptable, no support groups existed to help me deal with my problems. There were also no role models on which to pattern my behavior. I was very fortunate that my parents were enormously supportive and generous, with both time and money. They offered aid in any way they could. My father and mother even came to my home every single night to read the children a bedtime story, scratch their backs and tuck them in so they could still have a sense of family continuity.

The divorce was a vicious blow to my self-esteem. My husband had continually told me I was inadequate. Though I emerged from the experience coping well with the demands of a single life and single-parenthood, my ego never quite recovered from the beating it had taken. Yet, I was so busy showing myself and those around me that I was not weak or stupid or ugly that I never took time out to really consider what had gone wrong with the marriage. I never came to terms with the rage I felt. I never took the time to mourn the loss of a dream and the death of a marriage. In other words, in self-defense, I began to learn to sublimate stress. This mechanism worked, in a way; it got me through the immediate trauma. But years—and life-experience—later this mechanism had awesome repercussions.

In May of 1963, I was "fixed up" on a blind date with a man named Michael Blumberg, a man I would eventually marry and am still married to eighteen years later.

Our first date was like a dream. Bells rang. Light bulbs flashed. It was a case of love at first sight. From the first moment we knew there was some special chemistry at work between us. What followed was a romantic whirlwind courtship with a touch of realism to dampen the fantasylike quality. My children often accompanied us on dates. There were many times when Michael would fly to Cleveland to continue his courtship and we would spend the weekend nursing a sick child.

I married Michael at home, in March of 1964, in front of the fireplace.

We quickly began establishing new family patterns of living. We created a warm home and also traveled with the children often, especially on holidays. I worked part time and enlarged my volunteer activities, and I became very active in radio and television, appearing on shows on behalf of causes.

Because we spent so much of our time trying to create a new family unit and reassuring the children that the new family would be loving and supportive, we didn't have as much private time for establishing a strong relationship between ourselves as we would have liked. When opportunities arose that allowed us to travel together without the children, we looked forward to these excursions eagerly.

In October 1966, we traveled to the West Coast on one of

those jaunts. We had a wonderful time. I had never been to California before, and we did all the typical tourist things from dinner in Sausalito to riding across the Golden Gate Bridge at sunset to buying sourdough bread.

To save money we took the night flight home and arrived in Cleveland early on a Sunday morning. When we got to the house I sorted the mail, awoke the children, spent time with them and supervised their getting ready for Sunday School. Michael went to bed. I remember particularly that David didn't want to go to Sunday School; he wanted to come with me to drive Agnes to church, but I insisted he attend his regular Sunday School classes.

It was a beautiful sunny day. I felt wonderful. I dropped Agnes at church and started home, singing to myself as I drove along. Apparently, I was vulnerable to jet lag and the enormous fatigue that accompanied it. I passed out at the wheel of the car and slammed into a utility pole and tree. The tremendous impact as the car hit the pole caused my head to hit the steering wheel with enormous force. The top part of my skull above the forehead was nearly severed, and the metal rim of the old-fashioned horn tore away my skin and exposed my jawbone and carotid artery.

The passenger side of the car was totally demolished and anyone riding in the passenger seat would have surely been killed. How thankful I am that I insisted David go to Sunday School, because he would have been sitting in the passenger seat.

The injuries to my face caused extensive physical scars. One ran across my forehead from temple to part line and disappeared into the hairline. The other left a semicircular crease in the chin, which the children began calling my permanent smile. The severity of the injury to the mouth area necessitated an extensive amount of dental work, too.

But the worst scars were emotional. At a very early age I

developed a terrific inferiority complex about my appearance. I went through childhood and adolescence thinking I was not very pretty. I felt also that I wasn't as naturally intelligent as I wanted to be or, to some extent, was expected to be. So I always worked three times as hard as anyone else to prove myself and win approbation. I developed an outgoing, outspoken personality to hide the inferiority I felt.

My first marriage had done nothing to encourage me to feel good about the way I looked either. I became almost obsessive about my appearance after my divorce. This accident happened only two years into my marriage with Michael, at a time when I was still unsure of myself and of my relationship with him. Yes, the scars from the accident were far more than physical.

After I recovered from the accident, I began again living at a whirlwind pace, returning to parenting, working and volunteering again without pausing to assess the emotional wounds the accident caused. I pushed myself so hard that my face didn't heal properly or quickly. Finally, my doctors urged me to get away for a totally relaxing vacation, not one that combined business with pleasure for either Michael or me. Four months after the accident, in February 1967, Michael and I went to Jamaica for the first vacation either of us had ever taken solely for relaxation.

In Jamaica I was forced to take time to come to terms with the accident and the attendant physical and emotional scarring. But because I had waited four months, I had accumulated and stored a great amount of stress. I had continued following the same destructive pattern; when trauma entered my life, I didn't stop to deal with the resulting psychological pain.

On July 19, 1969, the same day that Neil Armstrong walked on the moon, I gave birth to a son. Stuart's birth was a perfect addition and helped complete Michael's and my relationship.

One month after Stuart was born, Cathy, David, Michael and I went to court to complete a delicate human process. Michael adopted Cathy and David. The timing could not have been more perfect. We became in name, as well as in fact, a united family. Peace returned.

In 1970 my father suffered a slight heart attack. As a result, he decided to heed this warning of his own mortality by accepting an offer to head Keren Hayesod (The United Israel Appeal), the fund-raising arm for the state of Israel. This decision meant that my parents had to move to Jerusalem, fulfilling a lifelong dream for both of them.

My parents were strong role models with regard to my volunteer activities. They were constantly involved in community projects themselves, building on a tradition summed up by the Hebrew word "tzedaka," a word meaning righteousness, charity and moral obligation. My father, in addition to presiding over a thriving law practice, served as law director of the city of Cleveland and assistant mayor before my birth. Before he left for Israel, he was the director of the Community Relations Board of Cleveland. My mother was a national vice-president of Hadassah and was constantly working on volunteer projects. Their dedication to philanthropic goals was a constant reminder that everyone had an obligation to serve the whole community. Since I grew up in this tradition, I devoted much of my time to volunteer work. It was only after my parents moved to Israel that I began working full time and merged both career and volunteering with the big "outside" world.

In 1972, I found a full-time career by accident in the field I had gained so much experience in during all my volunteer activities. The job was also a great blending of both public and private sectors.

As so often happens, I heard about the job from a friend at

a party. Because it was license renewal time, WIXY-AM/
WDOK-FM needed a community affairs director to beef up
their public-service broadcasting. Radio stations worried about
public-service programming at renewal time because that area
came under close scrutiny by the FCC.

I'm sure the general manager who hired me thought it wouldn't
be a permanent arrangement and once the license renewal
inspections were over I could be let go, but he failed to take
my determination into account. I stuck with the job. I used
the contacts I had made while volunteering to help improve
programming and expand the scope and the services of this
position. I found a mentor and learned as much about radio
broadcasting as I could. My efforts paid off. I am still with
the same FM station over ten years later, even though the
station management has changed countless times and ownership
has changed four times.

Thus, when serious illness struck in 1975, when I was forty,
I had a long history of high activity and much joy, but also
quite a lot of suppressed anxiety and intense stress. I was
growing as a woman—as a human being—but I was also getting
sick. It was only a matter of time until it all caught up with
me.

- 3 -

I don't think I exactly fit middle America's fantasy of an
ardent feminist. I was not the man-hating, bra-burning radical
feminist type. I really like men. I was and am a compulsive
housekeeper. Friends joke that I'm never without a sponge in
my hand to wipe away offending fingermarks. I am proud of
my home, my husband, my children.

In 1975, I didn't outwardly appear to be the kind of person
to get involved in planning the International Women's Year–
Cleveland Congress, but inside I knew that by serving the
International Women's Year (IWY) I could start righting some
of the wrongs that had been done to me as a woman, start
helping other women and perhaps help spare other women
some of the pain I had experienced, particularly during my
divorce.

When the United Nations designated 1975 the International
Women's Year, women in cities all over the country began
planning celebrations. We started planning the Greater Cleveland
Congress a year before its designated October 1975 date. I
seemed a natural to be selected for the steering committee
because I had proved my ability to raise funds after heading
the Women's Division of the Jewish Welfare Fund drive and
because for two years, in 1973 and 1974, I organized the
WVIZ-TV auction to raise money for the public-television
station. I had access also to extensive, diverse media contacts
because of my job.

By October 1975, the steering committee had just entered

14

the final stages of planning for the Cleveland Congress. I had completed most of my assignments for the congress, which included contacting celebrities, arranging for their appearances, and creating radio and TV publicity spots. I had also just received the little white card from my Ob/Gyn reminding me that it was time to schedule an appointment for my annual checkup and mammogram.

The mammogram turned out to be far from routine. Shortly after I returned home from the appointment, the radiologist who read the pictures called and asked me to return the next day. He wanted to repeat the mammogram. He had found three suspicious spots and wanted to recheck my breast with further tests. His reexamination confirmed his first appraisal. He suggested I consult my doctor and check into the hospital for surgery to remove the three minute growths and the surrounding tissue.

As had become my practice when confronted with a medical decision, I talked first with the family internist and good friend, Julian Kassen, an excellent diagnostician and a highly intelligent, cultured southern gentlemen. He talked to me and the other members of my chosen medical team, Sidney Sachs, my general surgeon, who had just become a specialist in diseases of the breast, and George Goler, my Ob/Gyn, who had delivered Stuart. They supported the radiologist's diagnosis. They told me I needed to have a lumpectomy to surgically remove the growths. I had quickly got my first crash course in cancer and the benefits of early detection.

When I entered the hospital, on October 11, 1975, a mere two weeks before the opening of the congress, I told my surgeon, Dr. Sachs, I would only sign the exploratory surgery form. I wanted to retain control over my body. I needed time to plan and consult with family and doctors if indeed the cancer had spread. I'd wait before I would sign the second consent form. No waking up in recovery without a breast for me.

15

When I did wake up from surgery I thought the scars I would have from removing three tiny little growths would be minimal, that my breast would look pretty much the same as it did before surgery. I didn't have much, but at least what I had was well-formed.

Not so!

I wasn't prepared for the ugliness of my breast or the dramatic change in its configuration. The nipple was in the wrong place. I felt misshapen, mutilated. When Dr. Sachs told me after surgery that the breast looked beautiful—from a surgeon's point of view, I guess—I decided from a woman's point of view that the man was crazy. He found it hard to understand my reaction.

Then I was disturbed even more because the pathologists didn't agree on a diagnosis. They couldn't decide whether the cancer had spread or whether they got it all and no further surgery would be needed.

My slides were shipped to Memorial Sloan-Kettering Cancer Center in New York for a verifying third opinion. The waiting was tormenting. But I was granted a reprieve. Memorial Sloan-Kettering Cancer Center sent word that no further surgery was indicated. No mastectomy necessary.

So I took my ugly, misshapen, mutilated breast and went home to prepare for the IWY Congress. I kept busy. I continued living, but once again, I didn't take any time to assess the psychological damage yet another scar had caused.

My friends told me how lucky I was. I knew they were right, but I had a hard time adjusting to the awful change in my body. I had to be more careful about the kinds of clothes I wore, and for the first time I felt self-conscious undressing in front of my husband, Michael.

Perhaps the thing that helped me heal psychologically was

lovemaking. I needed to feel beautiful, wanted, desirable, touchable. After some awkwardness in our first physical reunion after surgery, Michael and I quickly affirmed our deep sense of enduring love, in spite of the surgical changes.

Two weeks after surgery, I attended the private, opening reception for the participating celebrities and steering committee members of the International Women's Year–Cleveland Congress, October 25, 1975.

One of the highlights of the congress was the presence of First Lady Betty Ford at the opening session. As she started down the receiving line, I must confess I didn't look her straight in the eye, but straight in the chest. The whole time she approached me, I kept trying to figure out which breast was hers and which a prosthesis. I decided that the firm well-formed side was hers, the saggy shapeless one, the prosthesis. If I ever had to face a mastectomy, I vowed, I'd be sure and get myself a better prosthesis-maker. What a mistake! I learned later that the perfect-looking breast was the artificial replacement. I learned later also that it is very natural to inspect a woman's chest after learning she has had a mastectomy.

After what I had been through so recently, I was glad for the chance to meet Mrs. Ford and told her so. I thanked her directly for her openness, grateful she had shared some of her trials and fears with the nation. Her bravery made it possible for a lot of women to face the realities of breast cancer with more peace of mind.

Because we planners of the Cleveland Congress were determined that something endure from the inaugural convocation, we agreed that a women's center would best meet the goals set by the congress. From that determination the idea of a coalition, called WomenSpace, was born. It took us a few months of organizing to just sort out our politics and fears before we

17

could begin to work together, before we could really begin to hear one another. But we started to build our WomenSpace idea by idea. Our primary problem was that we needed a literal "space" to house ourselves.

At the same time as we were expanding, I became involved in another volunteer project, The Playhouse Square Foundation Renovation Project, which someday will become the second largest theater complex between Kennedy Center and Lincoln Center. Believe me, I knew every inch of real estate in the Playhouse Square area intimately. In the worst January snowstorm I can remember, I thought I had found the perfect location for WomenSpace in Playhouse Square.

Downtown Cleveland in early 1976 was a wasteland. No one came to the central city anymore. So most of the members of the coalition were appalled at my choice. But we were hurting financially and the rent was reasonable. The "space" that I found was thought to be too big, but it was cheap. I realized we would need to call on do-it-yourselfers from all over the area to make it habitable. I was willing to gamble because I believed in the coalition and in the reclamation of Playhouse Square.

In an executive session of WomenSpace, I felt for the first time in my career that I took a risk in public. I passionately worked to convince the board to consider the Playhouse Square location. I quoted an old Hebrew saying, "Change your place, change your luck." We argued. Oh, how we argued. Finally the executive committee agreed to move.

Then, thank God for a "good fire." The restaurant beneath our "space" caught fire one night, and since the fire damaged our proposed new offices, we shared in the insurance money. Everyone who had been concerned about turning the hellhole into workable area had to worry no longer. The insurance money went a long way toward restoring our space in a very short period of time.

18

MY ROOTS AND RECORDS

April 1977. Here I am in my garden room just before my world fell apart.

October 1940. A headstrong woman at age 6. Patterns for headstrong living start early.

August 19, 1981. My mother, Sylvia Shapiro, with Mayor Teddy Kollek of Jerusalem at the dedication ceremony naming a street for my father.

Reuven Rosenfelder

My father as world chairman of United Israel Appeal.

Carol Geddes

My father, Ezra Shapiro.

September 1977. My redecorated hospital room. Notice the Buddha from Bali. Who's superstitious?

Jonathan Lewis

Fall 1976. A family tradition. Here are my parents, my brother Dan and his wife Ellen, Michael, me, and all our children after building a Succah in our backyard.

May 1979. Cathy's graduation from Brandeis University. I was swollen, I was sick, but I lived to be there.

May 1978. A big month. Jane Fonda came to our home for the first benefit for Cleveland Women Working.

At my workplace: "All day. All night. All nice."

December 1980. Jane Fonda arriving at *Nine to Five*'s big benefit for Cleveland Women Working.

Agnes Peoples in our "soup kitchen."

September 1975. A moment with Betty Ford before the opening of the International Women's Year, Cleveland Congress.

February 1978. Dr. and Mrs. Billy Graham and my son, David, my handsome escort.

February 1978. A high point during chemotherapy when I received the Abe Lincoln Award. A red silk tunic covers my swelling shape.

Joseph W. Darwal

April 1979. Welcoming Joan Mondale to the Palace Theater.

Diane Hires

November 1981. Interviewing Betty Friedan about her book *The Second Stage* for my radio show.

November 1979. My family-of-choice at my 7:00 A.M., surprise forty-fifth birthday party.

February 1981. With Michael, listening to George Foley at the piano, the State Theater, downtown Cleveland.

Lucinda Hall Baker

April 1982. Celebrating. Headstrong.

As I write, WomenSpace represents twenty-five thousand women. The groups that actually occupy the ''space'' are Cleveland Women Working; Resource, an employment agency and career counseling center for women; The Helpline; and Domestic Workers of America. We who were insistent on seeing something grow out of the Cleveland Congress got what we envisioned. Our own dreams had come true. We expand each year. Our emphasis has shifted from physical protection to economic empowerment and a new focus on the family as we seek to grapple with women's issues of the eighties. We also established a 48.7 Club as a men's auxiliary group, the reverse of the typical social practice of a female auxiliary to a men's group; 48.7, taken from the percentage of men in the population, heralded a phase of the ''Second Stage'' discussed by Betty Friedan, a partnership between enlightened women and men for human advancement.

Thus, the phase of my first brush with cancer, with death, brought a period of solidification to my life. My career was booming, my volunteer activities were extremely exciting, my sense of myself as a woman had clarified, my family was fine. But I was sick—and getting sicker—with an invisible illness that I couldn't feel, but that was slowly destroying me.

-4-

The year 1977 was in many ways the most traumatic year of my life.

My father became ill again and had to be hospitalized with pneumonia in early February. Since he had accepted the post of chairman of the Keren Hayesod in 1971, he had circled the globe once every eighteen months recruiting leadership and raising funds for the state of Israel. It was a very wearing life for a man his age with a history of heart disease. It was not surprising that the rigors of his job, combined with his age and heart condition, caused him to get sick.

When he returned home from the hospital after his bout with pneumonia, he was still very weak. He tried to go back to work too soon and became ill again. My mother was concerned and called and asked me to fly to Jerusalem to help care for him. She knew how close we were and thought a visit from me might improve his spirits and help him regain some of his strength. In April, after our first family Seder without Grandpa singing the Hagaddah and leading us through the Exodus from Egypt, I flew to Israel to be with him.

I went to help care for him and give my mother a rest. We spent the first days of my visit, when he was still very weak, just touching and talking. In our conversations we seemed to take a journey through his life. It was natural to reminisce together. He even went over his scrapbooks with me, telling stories about the people on those pages and how they had touched his life. He improved gradually throughout my ten-day visit so that two nights before I left I was able to take him and my mother out to dinner at his favorite restaurant, Shemesh (meaning sun). The menu contained an entrée called "Steak Shapiro," named for him because it was his favorite dish.

The visit to Israel was a wonderful time for both my father and me. It was perhaps the first time in our lives together that he was able to see me as an adult with philosophies, passions, mature opinions, hopes and dreams of my own. We shared ideas, reviewed the past and grew closer than ever as we sat on his porch, where the hot Jerusalem sun tanned his forehead and gave him freckles, and walked in the streets of his beloved city. When I realized he was getting restless, strong and anxious to return to work, I knew it was time to return to my family in the United States.

On Friday, May 13, 1977, my family celebrated Shabbos, visited friends, came home and went to bed. At 1:00 A.M. I received a phone call from my mother in Israel. All she said was, "Come. I need you." I knew in that moment that my father had died. May 14, 1977.

I spent the rest of that long night calling my brother to tell him of our father's death and making arrangements to fly to Israel that same day. The government planned a state funeral for my father on May 16, on Yom Yerushalayim, the celebration of the anniversary of the reunification of Jerusalem.

My brother and I flew over together and during the interminable plane ride we reminisced and cried. That private chance to share our grief helped us to be strong for a public funeral and cope with the busy, grief-filled days ahead.

Flanked by our family and friends in Israel, we went to the public ceremonies given by the city of Jerusalem, both at the Jewish Agency building, my father's place of work, and then at an open funeral service for all the residents of Jerusalem. We carried his body through the streets of the city he loved,

21

past the open door of his synagogue, and drove to the Mount of Olives, where he was buried.

We remained in Israel for the shivah (the seven days of the official mourning) and we followed an Israeli custom of greeting people from 10:00 in the morning through to the end of each day, when a community service was held in my parents' home. We stayed up all night working to get my mother organized and her life in order. During that week my brother and I never slept. On the last day we went to the cemetery at 4:00 in the morning to say a private farewell to my father and then boarded the plane for the trip back to the States.

The summer of 1977 was a hectic one. First there were all the small duties one has to do after a family member has died. There were sympathy notes to acknowledge, my father's personal papers to go through and the formal memorial service given for him in Cleveland to arrange. My mother also stayed with me for six weeks that summer. She needed to be surrounded by familiar faces and places as she struggled to adjust to her new role. I also helped to prepare for the opening of the Palace Theater, part of the Playhouse Square reclamation project, carried on with my job and pursued my multiple roles as wife, mother and daughter.

I was much too busy to reflect on my father's death and what it meant to me. I was much too busy to properly grieve. Again, I dealt with stress by repressing it.

In August, Michael and I went to New York to see special friends of ours who were visiting from England. Addrianne and I are very much alike and are as close as sisters. A year earlier, she had had a mastectomy and at the time of her visit to the States was nearing the end of her chemotherapy treatments. She had come to New York for rest, rehabilitation and rebuilding, and she arrived the day after her final injection in one sequence of treatments.

Shortly after she arrived at the apartment she became violently ill. The arm that received the IV injection of anticancer drugs swelled to huge proportions, itched and turned black and blue. Finally, she was so disturbed by the reaction, as well as sick from it, that I called Dr. Kassen, in Cleveland, and asked for medical advice. I'll never forget her pain, nausea, discomfort and loss of hair. I will also never forget her courage, plucky attitude and indomitable will and energy to live.

The summer of 1977 was a nightmare. It was a season of trauma, frantic activity, of struggling to find the breath to keep going, of the sublimation of an enormous body of accumulated pain. Once again, true to the destructive pattern I had developed years earlier, I never took the time to deal with any of the stress that surrounded the pains. I concentrated instead on rushing from one activity to another, one obligation to another, one event to another.

My one great pleasure that summer was my involvement in planning another large community party to save a group of magnificent old movie theaters located in Playhouse Square in downtown Cleveland. The Playhouse Square Foundation scheduled a benefit to take place September 6, 1977, to ensure that the wonderful old buildings would not be turned into parking lots. The money raised would go specifically toward the restoration of the Palace Theater, once home of superb vaudeville entertainment. Many people involved in the restoration thought that any reclamation work would ultimately spur the revitalization of the whole downtown area. I was co-chairperson of the CHAIRity Event, where the device for fund raising was that each donor purchased a chair for the gutted theater, each chair bearing a small plaque with the donor's name on it.

23

In the midst of the preparations came the reminder card for my annual Ob/Gyn checkup and mammogram. I remembered Addrianne and shivered when I saw the little white card drop from a fall clothing catalog on a hot afternoon in August. I told myself that making the appointment wasn't urgent, that Jewish women for some reason didn't usually get cancer of the cervix, that people in my family generally died of heart attacks. Plus, I was scared. I didn't call for an appointment until all the preparations for the CHAIRity party were complete.

The examination began like an average, routine, secretly dreaded Ob/Gyn visit. I say ''secretly dreaded'' because I think most women feel vulnerable and somehow terribly undignified with their feet in the stirrups while a doctor moves around examining them, muttering commonplaces. Plus I had already had a scare two years before. My doctor, Dr. George Goler, happened to be a little bit different. In addition to being a big, comforting, affectionate man, he was a great raconteur, and that day he didn't disappoint me. He kept up a steady flow of cheerful chatter as he released me from the uncomfortable, awkward stirrups. He continued to regale me as he examined my breasts.

First, he palpated the ''good'' right breast and then moved to the left, the ugly, misshapen one. Suddenly the banter ceased. He frowned as he examined the left side. He seemed to pale. He lowered his voice and told me exactly what he felt and observed. The left breast contained a large lump, and the nipple was inverted.

God knows I should have noticed the changes in that awful, unsightly left breast. I had experienced the fear of cancer and knew about the benefits of early detection because of my lumpectomy two years before. I had devoted air time to the subject, when I interviewed my friend and the man who had performed the lumpectomy, Dr. Sachs. I, of all people, should have been aware. But I never examined the left breast after the lumpectomy.

24

I had a horror of touching it, let alone looking at it. I had a hang-up about my appearance and that hang-up nearly cost me my life.

Looking back I'm not surprised I ignored the telltale signs in the left breast that should have told me something was wrong. All the research about cancer I had done was for others, not for me. In the two years since my lumpectomy, I had become a super-denier, living my life intensely, totally sublimating what for me was the ultimate scar, the scar of a mastectomy.

After Dr. Goler finished his examination, he suggested that I get a mammogram as soon as possible. For some reason I delayed again. I told myself I wanted to complete the responsibilities I had undertaken on the CHAIRity benefit. I didn't go for the mammogram until two days after the opening of the Palace, September 8, 1977.

One thing that stands out in my mind about the mammogram, which I knew at a gut level was far from routine, was the sterile cheerfulness of the nurse. All the uncharitable things I thought about her stemmed from my own biases, as she carefully arranged my breast between the sponge and the Lucite frame on the X-ray platform to ensure correct exposure. She told me how "nice" my deformed left side looked. I was enraged. How could she possibly know or understand my feelings of revulsion? What I needed at that point was some semblance of sensitivity and understanding. She also took many more pictures than I ever remembered being taken before.

I went home to await the results: a real déjà vu experience, just like two years before, with the same sequence of events. An hour after I arrived home, the call came from the radiologist. The voice on the other end of the line asked me to return for further testing. Something wasn't quite right, I was told.

After my surgeon, Dr. Sachs, had received a set of the mammograms, he called me to his office for an examination.

25

While I sat in his waiting room I gazed around, trying to keep my mind off the forthcoming ordeal. I noticed things about the room that bothered me, things I had never noticed before. The room was painted a pale gray color and all the accessories were some shade of gray. The table and chair were done in muted tones of gray. I know gray is supposed to be a restful, calming color, but it has never been a favorite of mine. I always associated it with the day I went to court to get divorced. I was wearing a gray outfit.

On one wall there was a rack crammed with the usual assortment of magazines. One particular cover seemed to leap out at me that day. *Vogue*. *Vogue,* another small thoughtless act committed by an unknowing person, or so I reasoned in my fear and anxiety. With a mutilated breast or no breast at all, I couldn't wear most of the fashions advertised in the magazine. How did anyone have the nerve to leave that particular magazine in my line of vision. It suddenly became a symbol of all the things I thought I would probably never be again. At that moment, I really didn't know which was worse, losing a breast to cancer, or wondering if I did lose it, would I ever look chic or attractive again.

The nurse finally called my name and I went into the examining room and put on the cute little paper wrapper guaranteed not to cover my body but to rip and dehumanize. From thoughts and worries about *haute couture* to a paper bag. It was ironic; instead of focusing on survival, I deflected my fear and rage to *Vogue* magazine and paper gowns.

Dr. Sachs examined me as carefully and thoroughly as Dr. Goler had. He told me the truth, respecting my right to participate in any decision about my survival. He showed me the mammograms and allowed me to compare them to the ones that had been taken two years before.

An untutored eye could have detected the differences in the two sets of images. My eye was not untutored. The mammogram

26

showed almost the entire fibrous area of my left breast as a solid block. The tumor had totally invaded my breast. Dr. Sachs's needle biopsy confirmed the pictures' story. It was clear: I would have to have a mastectomy.

Dr. Sachs, a sensitive man who had children the same age as mine, spoke to my children at college and explained to them what was going to happen to me. He answered their questions and articulated their fears, fears about my dying that the children couldn't express. He spoke also privately with Michael, who went to Dr. Sachs's office for a visit after the workday. He spent a lot of time with Michael, reviewing the mammogram, discussing the surgical options, so that my husband really understood what was happening to me. Dr. Sachs even took the time to call my mother in Israel, to reassure her and answer her questions.

All these consultations and calls took place on Thursday, September 8, 1977. While my surgeon talked with different family members, I began to prepare myself and my family for the time I would be in the hospital.

I began to make lists. I listed menus, things I would need to take to the hospital, things my family would need while I was gone. You name it, I had a list for it. What a relief for a compulsive person like me to be able to list!

I also shopped on that Thursday. A friend gave me a robe with a pouch in front. She sensed I would need a place to rest my arm after the surgery. I bought some new slippers so that I would look presentable in the hospital. I did the marketing for the week that day too. And just to make sure I had plenty of changes of nightwear, I bought some new gowns and another robe.

On Friday I organized my work life. I spent almost the entire day recording tapes to ensure enough material for my radio show in my absence.

On Saturday, the day before I was scheduled to enter the

hospital, I was a hostess for a party in the park at Shaker Lakes. My main task during the day was to supervise the creation of a forty-pound Cheddar-cheese tree, a task I did with glee. While the party was in full swing, I cheerfully circulated among the crowds and helped with the serving.

On the morning of the day I was to go into the hospital, my daughter, Cathy, and I baked *taiglach,* morsels of dough filled with raisins and nuts, boiled in honey, the traditional sweet holiday delicacy associated with Rosh Hashanah, which was the next day. I felt very comforted and reassured about continuing the tradition. The familiarity of the ritual helped relieve the tension of the last few hours before I went to the hospital.

I made the lists, did the shopping, recorded for my radio show, concocted a cheese tree and baked the holiday morsels in an attempt to stay in control. If I stayed in control and didn't crumble or cry, I reasoned, I would make it easier for my family and perhaps even for me.

One of the things I had learned through my involvement with the women's movement was to take charge of my life. All of a sudden, some awesome, unexplained force had taken over my body. I couldn't feel it, I couldn't see it, but it was there. I thought that the more I fought it, the better my chances for survival.

I spoke no sentimental last words of farewell; no maudlin good-byes for me. I didn't write my last will and testament, and I didn't assign my treasures to my heirs because I wasn't going to die. Dammit!

The aberration that had invaded my cells was a test for me. It was a challenge. This accident of body chemistry was perhaps a nudge from God to keep human accounts current and values in order, to let my husband and my children and all my friends know what I thought about them; to make sure that those who touched my life, however marginally, knew I really cared about them.

Michael's feelings about what was happening to me during those few days between detection and surgery were hard to discern. He was shocked, of course, and very worried about me. But I think he was also angry with me. I was the compulsive careful one, I had done much research on breast cancer. How could I have been so careless about noticing the changes in the left side? He never shared any of his thoughts with me then, only later as I began to write the book.

On Sunday afternoon I packed my belongings and took my young son, Stuart, to my friend's house, and then Michael drove me to Mount Sinai Medical Center. After staying with me a short while, Michael returned to pick up Stuart and go home with him in order to provide comfort and reassurance.

After I checked in, I went through an extensive set of tests before I finally moved into my hospital room. I brought out a colorful pillowcase and an orange-and-yellow quilt to make the room more cheerful. I also dispensed the *taiglach* to staff who came in to take blood, "work me up" or consult with me. Even in a crisis, I couldn't stop entertaining or being a Jewish mother.

Surgery day arrived and with it the beginning of the Jewish year 5737. Lucky 7's, I thought. Michael walked beside me as they wheeled me to surgery. We kissed good-bye, but parted quickly. I knew this was essentially a private journey. It must ultimately be done alone, the fight for life coming from deep within. I tried with my eyes to assure him. I'll be there. I'll survive. You won't need to get another wife! Believe in me. I'll make it. I love you.

After four hours in the operating room, my surgeon removed the tumorous cancer-infested breast and all the surrounding nodes. When I awoke in my room, I could tell the news was good. I saw the smiling eyes and relaxed faces of family and staff. The first preliminary lab results indicated the surgeons had got all the cancer.

My room began to fill with luscious bouquets and gifts. One friend, David Blaushild, brought me a sculpture from Bali, a wonderful, dancing figure of a man with a round, protruding belly. Legend had it that anyone rubbing the belly would have good luck. Friends, family, the children and I jokingly rubbed the belly daily.

But who's superstitious?

-5-

When I woke during the middle of the first night after the surgery, a large nurse loomed over me. She was a heavy woman with flabby underarms and tightly curled hair. The sight of her hovering terrified me. As she took my vital signs she talked to me. Much of what she said barely registered in my groggy, befuddled state. But I was alert enough to realize that she was telling me that she too had had a mastectomy. I knew that all her talk and actions was motivated by a sincere desire to reassure me, but I was too sick and tired to realize that then. While she told me about her mastectomy, she reached inside the bodice of her white nurse's uniform and pulled out what looked to me like a shapeless rubber blob and wagged it in my face. My God, it was her prosthesis. That was the first time I had ever seen one. In my foggy state it looked horrible. I know she wanted to help a fellow sufferer, but I was too frightened and sick to understand. The awful incident gave me nightmares the rest of the night. When the morning nurse came to my room, I told her what had happened. I never saw the night nurse again.

The day after surgery all mastectomy patients attended a physical therapy and rehabilitation class. We walked to the class to start exercising. The room where the class was held looked like a dance studio with mirrors all along one wall. Class members stood in front of the mirrors while the instructors showed us some of the exercises that would help us regain muscle use and strength. We used the mirrors to gauge our progress.

Because so much muscle was removed during surgery, the simplest-looking exercise was tremendously difficult. One exercise called for putting the fingers of the surgery side on the mirror and then walking the fingers up the wall as far as we could. The goal was to be able to walk the fingers up the wall to a point well above the head. I was lucky to move my fingers shoulder high the first day.

The class was held every day of the ten days I was in the hospital. The nurses and other trained specialists that acted as teachers were a part of an unusual team. This team had met me before I had met them. They watched as I underwent surgery. These same people were the ones who brought me a pillow after surgery to support my weakened, aching left arm. The cancer team gave sustained understanding support, always available in our rooms or during classtime for nonjudgmental counseling and encouragement.

The kind of program I describe was a normal part of the routine at the great cancer research centers but not often available in a community hospital setting. Dr. Sachs, my surgeon, had studied how beneficial a continuing care program for cancer patients could be and fought to institute one at Mount Sinai. Care and support didn't stop when I left the hospital after surgery; the same people who watched over me in the operating room became the administrative aide, injecting nurse and guidance team during the ensuing years of chemotherapy.

My next encounter with a prosthesis was at one of the daily rehabilitation and therapy sessions. A Reach to Recovery volunteer dressed in a tightly fitting sweater came to our class. First, she told us to look at her and figure out which breast was real and which the prosthesis. As with Betty Ford, it was difficult to tell the real from the fake. Much to my horror, she then spread out on a table all the different sizes and shapes of prosthesis to chose from. After my experience with the well-meaning but insensitive night nurse, I wasn't prepared to look at myriad shapeless rubber blobs, some with nipples, some without.

I had a violent reaction once again and lost my temper with the volunteer. The problem was really mine. I still had drainage tubes under the tight bandages on my left side and the thought of putting anything else there was a painful one. Besides, I really hadn't had time to come to grips with the amputation of my breast. I wasn't ready to deal with the idea of a prosthesis or the prosthesis itself.

After the physical scars had healed, I apologized for my outburst. I learned in time to accept the new silicone appendage. Later, I even traded in my first prosthesis for a new model complete with a nipple! That was indeed progress for me.

Throughout the time of my stay in the hospital many close friends and relatives paid healing visits. It was natural for my brother to fly in from New York to check on my progress. We had always been exceptionally close. We never fought as children, always supporting and respecting each other. I always drew strength and affection from his calm, sweet, loving presence.Flowers, letters, zany gifts, crazy cards arrived reaffirming my importance to friends. It was crucial to me to receive calls, letters and visits while in the hospital. I didn't want to feel abandoned, discarded or cast off like soiled goods.

One week after my admittance to the hospital, on Sunday, September 19, I looked up to find my three physicians walking into my room. They appeared grim and foreboding to me. A shock ran through me.

They told me my tissue slides had been sent to a California laboratory for complete study and analysis, a routine procedure. But the message had come back that the cancer had metastasized. I had become a Stage II cancer patient.

My chances for survival were dramatically reduced.

Because the cancer had spread, I was told I would need aggressive chemotherapy to hopefully catch the one random cell that might have broken free even before surgery. That one random cell could spread the cancer. One small unseen cell could kill me.

My medical team bombarded me with facts, statistics and survival rates. One cell. More than three positive lymph nodes involved. If I didn't take chemotherapy, there was a 75 percent chance of recurrence, and I would have a 25 percent chance of survival. If I did take the chemotherapy, I would reduce the chances of recurrence by 75 percent.

Here were these men, my friends as well as my physicians, telling me facts crucial to my making decisions about my life and death. *I couldn't hear them.* I sat calmly while they talked, giving every outward appearance of attention, but I blotted out everything they said. I didn't hear their voices. I didn't see their faces. Their facts didn't apply to me. I had too many things to do, too much life left to live.

One reason I tried to studiously numb my brain to what they were saying was because I thought immediately of my friend Addrianne. A brief month before, I had seen her in New York, seen what havoc chemotherapy had wreaked on her body. I hated what it had done to her because I loved her. And God knows I didn't want the same thing to happen to me.

Dr. Kassen struggled to reach me. He knew I had seen the worst and been horribly frightened by it one short month ago. He kept repeating, ''What happened to Addrianne won't necessarily happen to you, Rena.'' Each anticancer drug has different side effects and Addrianne was taking a different treatment regimen than was offered in the United States. It was true; what had happened to her might not happen to me. But who knew, dammit? Who could possibly tell?

But I had no choice. I had to accept the verdict of chemotherapy if I wanted to live.

I had another problem to face. Before the surgery, I had asked my doctors to promise that they would tell no one if the cancer had spread, not my family, not my friends, not my colleagues. If I kept it secret, I figured, I had enough energy to fool the world. I didn't want my husband to know because for some convoluted reason, I was afraid the knowledge would jar our relationship. Maybe I could even fool myself.

The three doctors, Kass, George and Sidney, overruled me. They explained the rigors of chemotherapy and said I would need help and support for the coming ordeal. With my last wish foiled, I felt I had lost control over the entire situation.

They called Michael, who was at home with Stuart, and asked him to come to the hospital. I watched the pain on my husband's face as the doctors told him the news. How loving can hurt! After they left the room, Michael simply held me.

Perhaps the physicians were right. I was going to need all the love, support and help I could get. During the next few days, I experienced just how right they really were. Friends and family paid visits, which healed and soothed. One friend, a fashion designer from New York, brought me an armful of gorgeous new clothes to wear home when I left the hospital. Since I had come without a bra to wear home, she went into the bathroom, took hers off and left the bra, which I stuffed with a "poof" that a Reach to Recovery volunteer had given me. Her visit, in particular, restored some of my natural optimism.

- 6 -

The day after my three physician friends handed down their chemotherapy verdict, I was introduced to Dr. Richard Bornstein, the oncologist who would direct and supervise my chemotherapy treatments. His visit was the low point of my hospital stay, perhaps one of the lowest points of my life. I couldn't seem to get the image of Addrianne and what the chemo drugs had done to her out of my mind.

Dr. Bornstein fed me details of the National Surgical Adjuvant Breast Program or protocol. The N.S.A.B.P. was an experiment. Shots of anticancer drugs were given intravenously and anticancer pills were to be taken orally, five days in a row, every six weeks, for two years. He told me I was scheduled to begin treatment in a few weeks.

The experiment tested whether a three-drug regimen increased survival rates significantly over a two-drug program. Selection of which treatment group I would fall into, randomization, was made by neither me nor Dr. Bornstein, he explained. I would have to take my chances in a national pool. I wouldn't know until the day before treatment if I was in the standard or the investigational section.

What was I? A piece of meat?

What happened to me, Rena Blumberg, person?

I had no alternatives because my cancer had spread.

Dr. Bornstein gave me the consent form to sign—a white piece of paper that spelled out in precise, clinical, cold detail exactly what was going to happen to me. When I signed I was even required to have witnesses. I suppose I should have viewed it much the same way as signing other important documents, but the piece of paper had the power to affect my life in ways no other document ever had. The scrap of white paper was, hopefully, my passport to life. I signed, realizing, subconsciously, that I had condemned myself to a rhythm of madness that was to last two years.

I collapsed when Dr. Bornstein left, maybe because I listened, really listened this time to what chemo would involve. Maybe I fell apart because I couldn't stand the thought of losing my individuality in the investigational study. Maybe the signing of the paper brought the reality of what I was committing myself to home with force. All I know is the minute he walked out the door I let out a piercing wail from deep in my gut. I must have sounded like a mortally wounded animal.

As I screamed out my rage and fear, it dimly registered somewhere in my conscious that I had heard the awfulness of the sound I was making before. Then it hit me.

When I called my children and my brother to tell them of my father's death back in May, I heard each one of them make the same cry of anguish, rage and grief. Maybe I was not only grieving for myself, but also finally letting out some of the huge amount of pent-up grief I never got rid of when my father died.

An hour after Dr. Bornstein left, one of the members of the cancer support team came to my room. I found out later that a chemo nurse is always sent to the rooms of the patients soon after they are told of chemo.

Because the support team is so sensitive to the needs of cancer patients, they seem to appear at exactly the moment they are needed. They know when the awful news is finally absorbed by the patient.

After I had calmed down, I had many questions for the chemo nurse. I wanted to know how sick I was going to be while taking the drugs. Of course, there are no easy answers to that one because each patient reacts differently to the drugs. I wanted to know what side effects I could expect to have. She told me with assurance I would experience some hair loss and advised me to buy a wig. One of my biggest fears, of course, was not being able to lead the active life I was used to. I was very concerned about how I would fit my life into the chemo schedule, because for the next two years the chemo schedule would control my activities, not the other way around.

Even in moments of great stress, I think, most people have some pretty frivolous thoughts that assume monumental importance. My last major question for the chemo nurse was not earth-shattering, but important to me. I wondered if I could still sit in the sun and work on getting a suntan while undergoing chemo. She told me that sunbathing was perfectly acceptable in moderation. Was I relieved. If I was going to be losing hair and be sick, at least I could be tan.

Since my cancer had spread, I didn't have the options that many other women do. When the cancer has not metastasized, physicians usually recommend a year of preventive chemotherapy. The regimen isn't nearly as rigorous as the two-year program, and the side effects are minimal. Women can elect to skip the precautionary treatment altogether, but I don't think it's a wise decision. I had a friend who had surgery at the same time I did, and chose not to take chemotherapy. She died a short while ago. She might have died anyway, but to my way of thinking, it's just too big a gamble to take. At the time I had the mastectomy there were experiments being done substituting other forms of surgery and radiation therapies. At that point in my life I opted for cutting off my breast rather than worrying about the odd cancer cell floating somewhere in the remaining tissue, spreading the disease.

On the last night in the hospital, the young director of WomenSpace visited me. She brought me gifts from my friends and sisters who had shared in the creation of the WomenSpace coalition. Their choices of gifts for me were indescribably thoughtful. They gave me a large blouse, larger than my normal size, because they knew that I hadn't realized my left arm would swell. They sent a wonderful mobile of blue modern birds soaring free in flight. I was moved by their vision of what life could and would be for me. I was also touched by the money they spent on gifts, money from people who had little to spare, but who had chosen to share what little they had with me.

I left the hospital ten long, eventful days after the mastectomy. I gathered together my plants and presents and climbed in the car of a friend and was driven home.

The surgery signaled the beginning of a new life-style. I had to start weaving together the tangled threads of my life. I knew the pattern would be different. The chemo schedule would become a dictator. But I needed other areas of my life to return to normal as quickly as possible. I wanted no pity, just understanding and support.

I rested the afternoon of my homecoming so I could go to the synagogue to attend the Kol Nidre service, the special observance held on the eve of Yom Kippur, the Day of Atonement. I needed to be in our family pew with my husband and sons. Cathy, my daughter, had gone back to college.

The cantor intoned the opening notes, the haunting melody, the Kol Nidre, and I felt at one with my belief and at peace, not angry, because I was back in a setting that had nourished me through my life. I went to the synagogue for thanksgiving and reaffirmation. How proud I was as I walked up the aisle with my family to our seats. I used a large quilted envelope purse to support my left arm in place of the pillow I used in the hospital. No one knew. Only I knew the effort it took to smile and walk proudly, but it was important. It was crucial. With that action, I set my course. No anger, no fear, head up, close to the family. Out in public. To start the road to recovery I chose to begin in synagogue.

The first time any woman makes love is unforgettable But women experience many first times sexually: the first time after marriage, the first time following the end of a pregnancy and the birth of a child, the first time with a new important person in her life. The first sexual encounter after a mastectomy assumes incredible importance in many women's minds. Men may be afraid, but most women need the physical contact desperately.

Mastectomies leave ugly, painful psychological scars. Many women return home from the hospital feeling like a piece of damaged goods. The first sexual contact after surgery reaffirms womanhood and worth as a partner.

I experienced those feelings. Before I got into bed the evening I came home from the hospital, I went into the bathroom and put extra tape on my bandages to keep them from slipping in preparation for my "first time" after the mastectomy.

I also donned a nightgown. I asked Michael if he minded if I kept it on while we made love. I was extremely self-conscious about the bandages and the scars. His response showed his tenderness and understanding of me and what I had been through. He agreed and to this day I still wear a nightgown while making love. I haven't yet got over the self-consciousness I feel at my disfigured body.

Michael made love to me the way I think most men should if their wives have been through a similar experience to mine. He was patient. He touched and caressed me gently. He didn't rush foreplay. He seemed to sense that I needed time to feel good about my body again, and the way he could teach me to like myself again was to take the time and allow me to feel pleasures I was secretly afraid were lost to me forever.

He also seemed to know that I was still very sore from the

operation and that a slow easy approach would not only heighten sensation and excitement, but protect my body from any more hurts.

What surprised him when he saw the tears that rolled down my cheeks after I had an orgasm was that this special intimacy was the beginning of healing for me. His tenderness, understanding and patience as a lover helped me toward recovery. The miracle of my body's capacity to respond to passion in spite of what it had been through gave me courage for the days ahead.

I returned to work two weeks after the surgery. During that week I received notification that I was to be honored with the Southern Baptist Radio-Television Commission's Abe Lincoln Award, given for major contributions made through broadcasting to the quality of life in the city. The award is the equivalent of an Oscar and the highest honor I had ever received. It was very important to me to be able to attend the ceremonies in Texas and pick up the award in person. My station manager gave permission for me to take time off to travel to Texas, but I had to pay attention to the new boss in my life, the chemo schedule. I did go to Texas, but I realized that my chemo schedule was to become the controller of my life for the next two years.

Every week for the next few weeks after surgery I went to Dr. Sachs's office to have the mastectomy wound examined and drained. Finally, he removed the bandages and I had yet another scar on my body. It seemed to me that the history of people's lives can be read from the wrinkles on their faces and the scars on their bodies. The scars on my face I hid with makeup. The new scar I camouflaged with clothes. I decided a scar was a positive symbol, a sign of another chance. It was a reminder not to waste one day, to live each day as a celebration. I put the reality of the scar into perspective. It became less and less a priority concern. Living, surviving were.

– 7 –

In October, I began living with chemotherapy. I started treatment three weeks after the mastectomy. I couldn't understand why I had to start treatment so soon, without what I considered an adequate period for recuperation from surgery. Apparently, researchers had proved that adjuvant treatment is most effective when begun three weeks after surgery.

The first round of chemo was horrendous. I felt like I had been run over by a truck again and again and again. I was nauseated and not sure whether the nausea was from the toxic effects of the drugs or from fear at what was the new all-pervasive controlling pattern in my life. It was awful. I was given other drugs to counteract the effects of the direct treatment, and instead of relief, I got sicker.

This process of experimentation to find relief continued through the first few rounds of treatment. It was subtly suggested that I try marijuana for relief. It was by far the most effective substance to alleviate some of the side effects, but I did not like the fact that marijuana puts the vital center of the brain to sleep, which, in turn, activates nausea.

Finally, I decided to try to handle the side effects directly and not mask the horror. To some extent, this worked better. I knew what I was dealing with and could focus my effort. One aggravating feature was that the reactions were never the same during each chemo cycle. Some months the sickness built to a height at the end. Other times, socko . . . the worst came at the beginning and then the symptoms tapered off. It was the unpredictability that caught me off guard. If I could have planned and predicted, I could have armed myself and hung in there. The random nature of the violent illness kept me off guard, sick and in fear.

There were actually times I had to focus on not vomiting or having a diarrhea attack in a public place. I would freeze a smile on my face, try to listen, tighten my sphincter muscle, breathe deeply and fight for control. Looking back now I wonder how I ever did it, especially when I collapse over a flat tire or a broken appliance. To help get me through the normal crises of everyday living now, I try at these times to remember the enormous will I exerted then. Also, to be honest, there were deep dark black moments when I waivered and wasn't so sure I would make it. "We never cry in public" is a family motto, but believe me I cried plenty in private, especially when my body tricked me and eluded my efforts at discipline.

A time that I did lose control of my bodily functions comes back to haunt me vividly. Michael and I were attending a party in a public place. I had on a gorgeous dress. Suddenly, the cramping that always signaled the onset of diarrhea started. Then I felt the wetness between my legs as I sat in my seat. I excused myself from the table and moved to the bathroom as unobtrusively as possible. Once there I removed my clothes and undergarments. My underwear was soiled and there were telltale stains on my dress, too. I rinsed out all my clothes, wrapped the underwear in paper towels, discarded them, and climbed back into my wet dress. I sprayed myself with perfume and returned to our table. Michael had to take me home.

Any woman who has had a public accident during her menstrual cycle probably understands a little of the embarrassment and humiliation I felt. But there is something infinitely more degrading about having an accident when the bowels are involved. I never wore the beautiful dress or used that perfume again. It brought back too many painful memories.

During the first round of chemo, I learned about the search for veins, the five roadways, the five veins needed for treatments five days in a row. The same top surface of one hand must be used because a patient can only take treatment through the hand on the good side, where there are nodes, not on the side where the mastectomy has been done. I discovered more color combinations of black and blue than I ever imagined. Not that the nurses weren't good at administering the drugs. The bruises were just another fact of treatment. When I speak now and a person approaches me after the lecture and I see her black-and-blue hand, I get a sudden wave of nausea remembering the chemotherapy injections.

After the first round of chemotherapy, I was invited to speak on the patient/doctor relationship at a symposium sponsored by the American Cancer Society. Other panelists included some real heavies: an outstanding oncologist, a noted radiologist, and my friend, Dr. Sachs, the surgeon. The society wanted me to provide the human touch, talk about the niggling realities of coping. Most cancer patients develop coping strategies suited to their life-styles and temperament. I addressed myself to the issue of the patient as coper and a consumer. I talked about the fact that every patient has a right to know the truth and has a responsibility to participate actively in her or his treatment. No patient should remain passive and accepting; as Norman Cousins said in his book *Human Options,* "Patients who have a fighting spirit and who won't accept a negative verdict are far more likely to improve than those who responded with stoic acceptance of feelings of hopelessness and helplessness!"

It was a sobering decision to make, this going public and advertising the fact that I had cancer. Would it affect my family or work relationship? Would people be afraid to touch me for fear of "catching" cancer? Did people look me in the chest and try to figure out which breast was real and which was not? I decided it just did not matter. Fighting the myth-beliefs and misinformation helped me. As I fought for my own life, I fought for the dignity and rights of patients who came to hear me speak.

Other invitations to speak poured in. That same year, I headed the suburban cancer drive for the Cleveland area Cancer Society. Looking back, the personal crusade I made with my money and my mouth was another division recruited for the big fight.

Another worry I had after "going public" and then entering the chemo schedule on my daily calendar was how would I be able to keep my job. Surely I couldn't consider the two years of chemo vacation time, and sick time hardly described the ongoing process of poisoning. In a quick-changing, fast-paced business like radio communications, how could I carve out a special new niche that could be beneficial to the station and possible for me?

I thought about it and then did something brave out of necessity, which I encourage everyone in a similar situation to do. What I did represented coming full circle from my private desire for secrecy about my illness. I went to our general manager and told him honestly and openly what the chemo process was and how the schedule worked. Together, we set up a flexible working schedule to accommodate my needs. When I was well, I recorded double time. I often worked at home in bed, near the bathroom. I figured, if I hyped my voice with vigor, how would anyone know where I was calling from when I returned calls? The important thing was that each phone inquiry be returned promptly and effectively.

The staff in the office was sensational. They always covered for me. Their response to a caller was that I was out and I would call back shortly; usually all calls were returned in a few hours. People were always flattered at our polite handling of their needs. At all times I kept faith with our audience.

The library researchers at the public library got me materials for the in-depth preparation of my interviews. By lying down while I did research, I saved energy and kept on working. When recording, I drank water constantly to keep my voice from cracking and showing the drying effects of the drugs. Radio was a blessing, because the audience could hear the image in their mind that I created verbally. They didn't have to see the stark reality.

One radio executive, new to the station, who knew about my treatment schedule, took me to lunch one day to get information on his new territory. After coffee, he thanked me for my advice and said he was sorry that we couldn't become friends. I asked why not. He said his mother had died of breast cancer and he couldn't invest in a friendship with me because I might die, too, and he didn't want to expend that energy again. He protected himself at peril to my wounded soul.

The period of chemotherapy is a blur, with some highs and small victories, and lows of terrible nausea and illness.

One high exhilarating experience came in February 1978 on a Wednesday, Thursday and Friday right before my fourth treatment. I felt lucky that the prescribed scheduling permitted me to attend the event that turned out to be one of the highlights of my life. Since my husband had an important business meeting already scheduled, my son David, who was on winter break from college, volunteered to join me as my escort to Texas for the Southern Baptist Award ceremonies, where I was being given the Abe Lincoln Award for excellence in broadcasting.

The ceremonies were formal and lavish. I went to Fort Worth early to attend the business meetings. I had bought a red silk tunic to wear over turquoise silk pants to cover my expanding body. Already, the anticancer drugs, which contained steroids, were causing me to retain fluid and gain weight. I wore bright red, which I knew made me feel ravishing. For that one night, I took off the scarf I had been wearing to cover my balding head and found a lady barber in the hotel (since there was no beauty shop) who teased the remaining hairs on my head and helped me look presentable.

The meetings had been interesting and now I was dressed and ready, waiting for David. He arrived perilously late due to an ice storm. He jumped into his tuxedo and was ready in the nick of time to take me to the reception for the honorees and Billy Graham. While we waited backstage in line to go on the stage and be announced, a telegram was read aloud to the group from my mother in Jerusalem. The multimedia presentation on each of us was spectacular. The elegance of the experience, shared intimately with my wonderful son, was a glowing image I carried with me and summoned for reassurance and sustenance.

As the treatments continued, my body began to swell. I didn't fit the traditional image of the cancer patient, just as I had never fit traditional images before. I was not getting thin to the point of emaciation, nor was I sallow. People asked me if I was eating myself to death. Because the medicine stimulated appetite, I figured I was eating for my life. I decided if I was going to be fat, I could at least look good.

Each day I sailed forth, colorfully made up and dressed. I resisted the temptation to wear dark colors that would visually reduce my bloated appearance. Instead I opted for bright, flowing, loose, comfortable outfits to cover my girth. I added large pieces of jewelry, feathers or flowers near my neckline to draw attention away from my swollen belly to my face.

Besides getting fat during the chemo treatments, I experienced wide mood swings. I always prided myself on my discipline and self-control, but as treatment progressed my emotions had less and less stability. I managed to maintain a calm facade in public, but in private I sometimes cracked in funny ways. My family recognized the signs and labeled my behavior, particularly the last week before chemo treatments in any interval, the "chemo crazies."

I cleaned with a vengeance. No fingermark or spot of dust was too small to be overlooked. All work had to be done meticulously, perfectly. Plus, I demanded as much of those I loved as I did of myself. I found myself setting unrealistic goals to prove to myself I could still function. I had to demonstrate that I didn't have water on the brain, as I had all over the rest of my body. I wanted all projects completed, maybe because during the week of the actual treatment I felt I might drop off the face of the earth. I constantly doubted whether I could ever be able to return to normal life.

Those closest to me helped me perpetrate a fiction for the outside world. They forced me to abandon false pride and admit I needed help and to ask for it. It was a frenzied, intense time for everyone. For a willful, proud, independent person like me, perhaps the hardest thing to do was ask for help, and help I needed in many ways.

I turned for help to my father's brother and sister-in-law, Uncle Manny and Aunt Helen. They subtly and quietly continued the family tradition of pitching in in time of emergency.

Aunt Helen, a saintly woman, had a lifetime tradition as a helping person. She worked to help retarded persons have a better life and even taught prisoners at the county jail in an effort to ensure their parole. When family members were stricken, she dropped everything to give full-time assistance.

Uncle Manny carried on the all-for-one tradition of the Shapiro side of the family. I grew up thinking all bright and marvelous people in the world were somehow related to me. My terrific grandmother, "Bubbie," was a woman way ahead of her time. She revered learning and her handsome husband, Osias Shapiro, who was a respected rabbi. She ran a stogie factory above their house and raised her children, quite successfully, below. Each of her sons became a professional. Everyone worked and brought their money home to the kitchen table. Each brother was given all the education he needed, in sequence, with all assisting him at his moment. My father became a lawyer literally to replace his eldest brother, who died in 1920 (and had been a lawyer). The others were an ophthalmologist, a dentist and a pharmacist. My father's sister became a teacher, in those days *the* respectable, safe position for a woman.

Every Saturday of my early life, I spent at Aunt Helen and Uncle Manny's home with all the nieces and nephews. At their home we all learned music. If I wasn't at one of Aunt Helen's two pianos, I was in her kitchen eating or outside climbing the apple tree across the street. No discipline problems, no amusement problems. To me, Aunt Helen and Uncle Manny were the central force of this world.

From the beginning, Uncle Manny and Aunt Helen drove me for every single treatment cycle for two years. At the same time I was going to chemo, my father's sister, Aunt Sarah, was having treatment, too. Aunt Helen and Uncle Manny drove us both, often two trips in the same day.

On the first day of treatment I could usually manage on my own, but not the rest of the week. Too often, the medicine had made me sick, almost right away. One day I got sick in the car. Uncle Manny began to sing some old Yiddish melodies he and my father had sung as boys. He instinctively sensed the proper medicine for me. He seemed to know that the songs gave me the strength of my heritage and brought the image of my father close to me. Both were always a comfort.

When I would come home from treatments, already sick, nauseated and ready for bed so no one would see me, Aunt Helen headed for Stuart's room. She would stay with him when he came from school, help with homework, hear his day's tales, lose to him in cards and games, and keep his life smooth by covering him with attention, abundant affection and love.

With a mother's modesty, I must say Stuart was an angel, and an accomplice. He was vaguely aware that something was wrong, and that I needed rest more often than he was used to seeing me do. But he never really understood what was going on and how it could affect him. His world was kept as sane as possible, and because he was so good and cooperative the planned normalcy worked. He was remarkable in his gentleness and thoughtfulness as he tried to play quietly and take care of himself. I don't think he ever realized that other mothers weren't quite like me. Later when I discussed what had happened to me with him, he felt good about his positive role and proud of his help. What might have been threatening and fearful was turned around to a positive growth experience.

Agnes Peoples, our housekeeper, who had presided over our house for many years with absolute power and integrity, gave her special brand of help, too. She is a quiet person, but a strong person. She, too, had survived cancer and well understood the challenges. Agnes was respected as a church member, speaker and organizer. I sometimes felt that God had sent her to help me at crucial moments. She arrived from Alabama when my first husband left. She remained through all, living nearby, just down the street, coexisting with me in an unusual partnership. Her friend Lee came to help occasionally, since neither Agnes nor I was in top physical shape. What sustained us both was Agnes's motto, drawn from her deeply religious approach: "God never closes a door that he doesn't open a window."

Extraordinary friends in my extended family-of-choice also helped with everything from Sabbath dinners to holiday observances, to small human kindness that spared me and allowed me dignity and an extra measure of energy reserve. I constantly had to evaluate my energy reserve and priorities. It was hard

50

to swallow my pride and say, "I need you." But I had a wonderful surprise. People didn't mind being asked when the need was genuine. I had been afraid that by asking I would lose close friends, and I would lose their respect. I thought that only by giving could I keep relationships. Thank God my insecurities were proved wrong.

Every person who touched my life helped. It was tough to learn a new role, to receive graciously and unashamedly. On my agenda now is to find countless small ways to repay these gentle, good souls. I have learned that while I cannot always repay them directly, I can do acts in kind for new people in stress, and in need, and extend my hand and open my heart, preferably before they have to ask.

After I learned to ask for help, I developed a protective fiction that I used with my friends. I remembered the lesson of a favorite professor at Brandeis who taught me "Joy is binding, grief is separating." Mindful of this lesson, we would converse in a special code. For example, their question: "How are you?" My response: "Fabulous." This meant good. Question: "How are you?" Response: "Terrific." This meant reasonable. Question: "How are you?" Response: "Fine." This meant awful. They learned to read my signals so that I never had to complain, and we could communicate the truth through humor and merriment, yet let me keep some semblance of pride.

On the other hand, I was totally honest with my physicians, who could barely believe all the side effects that were happening to me. I also told the truth to other patients in my chemo group, because in our honesty we helped one another. I did not always tell the truth to my husband and my children. I really did not want to frighten them. I never wanted them to have a sense that I might die; I wanted them to believe I would live. For the outside world, I kept my posture. I used my words "fabulous," "terrific" and "fine." Let them figure out how I managed. I was going to be a survivor.

Michael had a hard time facing the fact of my cancer and I suppose the possibility of my death. He only showed it in one passive way during the period of chemotherapy. He never once took me to the hospital for treatments, always pleading business as an excuse. I sensed his pain, but I didn't find out until later how he felt. He said that he never wanted to witness the treatment scene because as long as he never saw it happening in the hospital, he could deny the whole thing. Also, he said he knew I would survive and he was confident of my ability to triumph. Actually, I found myself protecting him and other members of the family from some of the grim realities. Thus I participated in the fiction and the denial. I permitted those who wanted to deny, to deny; those who wanted to put their heads in the sand, to do so. I gave off more energy and tried to be a super-accomplisher and to keep doing all the roles I had, in the best possible way. I found that I never wanted to force someone into a role that they couldn't accept, and today I do not regret it. I allowed each person to set her or his own boundaries.

I found out about my son David's feelings after I asked him to drive me to and from the hospital for treatment one day. I showed him the physical setup, introduced him to the nurses and some of the fellow patients. The next day David was crabby and out of sorts, which was unusual for him. My becoming ill and possibly dying were a personal affront to him, and what made it worse, he felt guilty for feeling that way. Since I had read that this reaction was normal and was aware that Michael had experienced it too, I was able to explain to him that this was normal, acknowledge his feeling, diffuse his angers and tell him that in spite of the strange response, I loved him.

The chemo crazies took another form, the "chemo blues."

The blues hit me hard when I'd go for treatment and find someone from the group had had a recurrence. I fought hard to keep fear at bay, but when someone disappeared from the group, I had to face the reality of that person's possible death, and then maybe mine.

I alternated between periods of hedonism and altruism in coping with the blues. Everything edible went into my mouth. What did it matter? I was already fat, so why deny myself? Anyhow, I might die tomorrow.

I resisted the urge as often as possible to stay in bed, pull up the covers and hide, for I thought that would be the ultimate defeat. I came down each morning with my hair brushed, a little rouge on to give me some color. I recorded in my diary on the last day of chemo that I never once missed a morning when I got up to give my family breakfast. That became a symbol for me. There were times I was in a wretched condition, but I always came down to slice a grapefruit, to help with the toast, to check for clean fingernails, to kiss each person good-bye and wish them a good day. Keeping my place at the core of my family helped me combat the blues.

When I hit a perilously low state I had strange fantasies. Black humor was a release. It was an incentive to live, so I worked out my fears in a fantasy, but these fantasies were maudlin. I thought that when and if I died, who would be my husband's new wife? I was embarrassed and felt guilty about what I was thinking, but many women combating chronic illness had fantasies like mine. I heard of one woman dying from cancer who actually made up a list of friends for her husband and recommended them in order of her preference.

Nighttime became my enemy. During the daytime I could hold my fears and emotions in check. During chemotherapy, my nights seemed as busy as my days. The clock mocked me; I kept looking at it but the hands never seemed to move. A rush trip to the bathroom always left me wide awake.

After a while, I learned to not fight the state of restlessness and make use of it in a positive way. I actually cleaned drawers sometimes. It was mindless and productive, but it tired me out.

If I chose to stay in bed, I would prop a flashlight up on my shoulder and read magazines or poems. Something light in weight to hold and short in time to cover seemed to work better. I didn't have the energy or the concentration to take on a heavy, serious literary novel at 2:00 in the morning, but poetry was a release. A poem kept my fantasies in motion and diverted my anger and impatience.

When all else failed, I wrote letters to friends or just notes on a yellow pad. The yellow pad was indispensable. When waves of despair threatened to overwhelm me, I divided the paper in half and wrote out reasons for living on one side and reasons for dying on the other. After a short period of self-pity, I made sure the reasons-for-living list was longer. I chose something positive to focus my fantasies on and stayed in bed until I fell asleep or until it was a reasonable time to rise and start a new day.

-8-

The Oncology Department was located in the nether regions of the hospital, far enough away from the mainstream of hospital life so that it wouldn't advertise the vulnerability of the medical profession when faced with the reality of life-threatening disease, or so it seemed to me. Cancer meant death and dying to most people, so we were segregated from the masses into a little colony. It was a dreary place, too. The walls were painted a hospital drab. It was a physical place of inhuman contact; human amenities were missing. The one toilet was impossible to get to because it was located inside the treatment room. God knows, if there was anything a chemo patient needed it was a conveniently located toilet.

Yet it was also a personal place of human contact, where cancer-consciousness raising was practiced, where patients could openly share information about symptoms, side effects, prognoses, give advice and ask questions. We who came for treatment every day for one week out of six became a tightly knit little group. That's why it was so devastating when one of the group had a recurrence or a sad episode in her life.

The most frequent topic of conversation was about chemo side effects. To put it quite simply, chemicals used to search out and destroy that one random, irregular cell that might be floating free don't discriminate. The life-giving poisons attack healthy cells, too. The destruction of viable cells causes the gut-wrenching, demeaning, often embarrassing side effects. And no one really quite understood the devastation of these drugs except the people in our chemo treatment group.

Most doctors won't enumerate all the possible side effects for patients before they start treatment. Each patient reacts to the drugs differently, so the effects are hard to predict. Physicians are not foolish. They don't want to list potential problems that might deter people from taking the life-giving drugs.

So we learned together about nausea, which was ever-present for all of us. The dictionary defines nausea as ''a stomach disturbance characterized by a feeling of the need to vomit, strong aversion, repugnance, disgust—from the Greek *nausia* (seasickness) from *naus, ship.*'' This and any other dictionary definition are totally inadequate when describing the nausea as it related to chemotherapy drugs. This nausea defies description. There were no specific words gross enough to capture the humiliation and desperation connected with the feelings. It was a private hell. No other person could share, help with or relieve it. Other drugs could mask or diminish nausea, but they all carried their own side effects. Nausea was an unremitting source of disability. It was heightened by intensified waves. There was no time off from nausea. True to the definition, the locus seemed to be experienced in the stomach, but it consumed and affected the whole being.

A related problem was ''metal-mouth.'' Metal-mouth was occasionally relieved by sucking hard candy or eating ice cream or sherbet. I brought in a fancy container for hard candy to share with other patients in their search for relief from metal-mouth. I was back to redecorating yet another area of the hospital. Normal tastes were distorted tremendously.

Smell went haywire. An odor that had once been pleasant and aromatic, and previously programmed in the sensory computer to give pleasure, could suddenly trigger a violent reverse reaction. No warning was given for the switch in signals. It might happen once but not again. Because of this reaction, I didn't need a second experience or warning. The aroma of garlic destroyed me, but so did other ostensibly harmless smells like Brussels sprouts and even a perfume I had loved.

Unpredictability, the loss of personal control, the sweating, and the projectile vomiting, all kept the nauseous person scared, tense, nervous and off-balance. Unwell from chemo, a person lost stability and balance because of uncontrollable body responses.

Vomiting reduced anyone to a terribly low common denominator and a wretched level of survival. The rejection of material, the wretched reversal of ingestion destroyed ego, image and dignity. The final defeat was when multiple systems ceased functioning properly, simultaneously. Trying to deal with diarrhea and vomiting at the same time led to the juggling of bathroom equipment, accidents, tears, exhaustion, despair and eventually hysterical laughter at the gross nature of the situation.

When nauseous, some people couldn't eat at all. They took in small amounts of barley water, drops of ginger ale or tea to keep from becoming dehydrated. They of course got thin, but the women in my group all gained weight.

One reaction to nausea and metal-mouth was hunger. Strange, isn't it? We were eating to live, we were trying to fight by building up strength. We were also in a pathetic search for taste that would supersede the metal-mouth residual flavor. The nurses advised us to try the following foods: cola syrup on shaved ice, potatoes, rice, popcorn. Ha! Terrific for weight watchers. But at this time we were willing to try anything for a moment's comfort and relief.

There was no glamour, no heroics in the fight against the insidious, eroding effects of nausea. The memory of chemo, unlike labor, doesn't fade, and it isn't forgotten. The memory remains clear and helps keep us vigilant and assertive in the fight for survival.

The syndrome response never left. When I was watching a "60 Minutes" TV segment about children with cancer who were on chemotherapy, I saw them as they were receiving treatment drugs through the familiar needle, and I was overcome with nausea. The sight of chemo drugs flowing through the needle triggered an immediate violent response.

We learned many things in our treatment cycle group. We learned that with certain drugs, all hair fell out, and with other drugs a portion of it fell out. Hair became wispier, dry and brittle, like stringy Brillo. The chemo nurses advised patients to buy wigs to match their hair color before beginning treatment. It was interesting to note that no one chose a wig in another color. So much had changed. We didn't want to change our hair color, too. It would just add another set of complications with which to deal.

A double standard surfaced. Most men who lost their hair didn't buy wigs. They coped by wearing jaunty caps, or they went bald. It was acceptable to go out looking like Yul Brynner or Telly Savalas. The women weren't as fortunate. Few stores provided private places for trying wigs on. Another humiliating factor. If a bald woman tried on a wig in public, other well women wouldn't even touch the same wig. Shopkeepers were not sympathetic to the plight of a bald-headed woman and did not encourage them to shop at their establishments because it was bad for sales.

Many women tried remedies other than wigs. I, for one, wore soft, terry caps at home, so I would look better in front of my family. I also had my hair cut and conditioned by an expert cosmetologist. He helped save the hair I had and made me feel good about myself in the process. Add him to the list of caring, supportive people.

Our little group learned that the drugs did funny things to other fast-growing cells, for instance, to fingernails. This was a special problem for me because I took pride in my hands. My father had set great store in having clean fingernails, and we were taught to take care of our hands. I loved wearing rings and other adornments, and found it hard when my nails were cracked, split and broken off. I also worried that a nail torn off on the left side, my mastectomy side, would cause infection.

During the rehabilitation process, we were taught not to cut the cuticles on that hand, and to be very careful of infection. We learned not to shave under that arm with a sharp razor blade, but to use instead a plastic Flicker shaver, which wouldn't cut or bring infection. We always had to worry about infection because there were no nodes left on the mastectomy side to fight disease.

To keep my fingernails from literally tearing off at the nail bed, I test-marketed for a friend a wonderful new product called Gluematic. The glue helped the nails grow out to at least the edge of the finger. Well, this was a new low or rather a hysterical high for me—keeping the body intact with super glue.

In the hall, our chemo group did what amounted to postdoctoral research in vitamins. Since little was written or known about which vitamins worked and what we should take, we all studied up and read as much as we could. We shared information hoping that through proper vitamins we could build up what was being destroyed. We always checked all of our research with the doctors. Many of us tried and continued to add vitamins to our list, like Bobby Riggs, so that we could in some way feel we were combating the destructive force.

We learned also about "dry eyes." I never left the house without "liquid tears." If I did, I would get a scratch on the cornea from excessive dryness, and the pain in my eyes was searing. I wouldn't be able to open them. Several times I had to call my ophthalmologist, who met me in the emergency room, anesthetized my eye, and put a patch on it until the corneal scratches healed. Twenty-four hours later I could open it.

Most of the time my eyes felt like I had rocks in them. In a theater or a smoky room, I had to continue using drops throughout the evening. My son Stuart was frightened when I had to wear eye patches. To him they indicated the visible sign of trouble and he was embarrassed by my somewhat piratical appearance. If I awoke in the middle of the night, there were times I had to reach for the drops. I couldn't open my eyes to see the clock until I used them.

Fatigue was the most difficult aspect of chemotherapy for me to deal with. Unlike loss of hair and nausea, I did not expect it. Since I'm a normally energetic person, this was particularly demoralizing.

Fatigue from chemotherapy was not like a normal loss of energy. It was heavy. It came on swiftly. It was like a bulk weight, bearing down on weak shoulders. To anyone who has not experienced the onslaught of toxic drugs, the feeling is hard to convey. I became moody, trearful and frustrated because of fatigue. In all the battles I fought, fatigue was a formidable foe that required enormous energy to overcome.

On a practical level, if at home, I could often sneak off for a twenty-minute rest on my bed, with my legs up on a pillow, just to find enough energy to carry on. Sometimes at work I closed the door to my office and lay on the floor in the dark to relax my body and allow myself to dig deeper to find an ounce of extra energy to refresh and permit me to stand up and walk. Fatigue made us all too tired to talk or sometimes even too tired to hold a pencil. It was an invisible enemy, stripping the chemo patient of resources necessary for daily living.

I delighted in calling chemo "poison." To me, calling it what it really was—or seemed to be—made it easier to deal with.

We chemo patients suffered general aches and pains, too. We couldn't seem to find one comfortable place on our bodies.

Our weight might shift as much as five pounds a day. That kind of fluctuation was unsettling and scary. I tended to focus so hard on fighting the pain that I would miss words spoken to me. A new worry came to my mind then, and that was just it, *my mind*. Was I losing mine? Was I becoming prematurely senile? As if all the side effects weren't enough, add a catalog of constant colds, earaches and sore throats.

I felt like Typhoid Mary.

Before each treatment cycle we chemo patients were required to have blood tests: one at midpoint, the three-week mark, and another the Friday before the Monday madness began. A blood count, a testimony of destruction, was determined and the number found indicated the dosage in the next round of treatment. If the white count was above 4.0, everything was fine. If the count dropped to between 2.5 and 4.0, you were given half a dose of the chemicals. If the white count fell below 2.5, no treatment was given during that protocol period.

Three times my blood count dropped very low. It happened at three important times in my life, toward the end of my course of treatments. The chemo dose was cut in half. I didn't feel nearly as sick, somehow, knowing I was on a reduced dose. My head conquered the side effects and I was able to travel each time to a grand event.

In April of 1979, I had treatment from the second to the sixth and then left immediately for Memphis, Tennessee, for the wedding of the son of my friend Addrianne. My mother flew in from Israel to join us for the wedding festivities.

The night before I left I set the Seder table in the dining room for twenty-three people so that it would be ready for our Passover ceremony and dinner when we returned the next week. I covered all the special dishes and the banquet layout with a huge sheet, and off I went. Even without chemotherapy, this would have been a terrific feat of preplanning. By setting up my objectives and doing lots of preorganizing and list-making, I was able to participate in all the joyous events.

Around this period, an older woman in our group was coming to the end of her cycle. She was so sick after the last round that she was unable to attend her grandson's wedding. I thought it terrible for her and her grandchild. Her inability to attend her grandson's wedding spurred me on to grab control, to plan ahead to achieve my daily goals. The whole battle had to be kept in perspective. I was fighting to live and conquer a disease and all the while participate in the daily happenings that constitute the essence of a life.

The second time my blood count dropped was when I went for my routine test shortly after Joan Mondale had been visiting Cleveland to present a Creative Arts Award. This was a particularly poignant time for me because one recipient, a good friend of mine, was brought to the ceremony at the Palace Theater from the Cleveland Clinic hospital in an ambulance. He forced himself to stay alive. The moment of receiving his award was his incentive.

When he returned to the hospital, the life supports were discontinued at his request and he died of cancer's ravaging effects two days later. His bravery and tenacity drove me on. Each act of bravery and heroism kept me headstrong and fighting.

My next treatment in May 1979 was mercifully reduced to half because of the low blood count. I flew to Boston and Brandeis University to be with Cathy, at her graduation. Again with a sliver of extra energy because the chemicals had been reduced.

Cathy had campaigned for me a year earlier to help me be elected an alumnae term trustee for five years, and this was the first year of my tenure. I was given the honor of speaking during the commencement festivities. I was assigned Cathy's departmental mini-commencement ceremony preceding the university exercises. It was the thrill of a lifetime to deliver my message to my accomplished daughter, Cathy, her classmates and their parents, and then to stand in the receiving line with her professor and personally hand her her college diploma, which she had earned with honors.

The Monday when the first treatment of the week was given, a certain ritual was followed. First, the humiliating weigh-in on a scale that stood in a hall in full view of everyone. I suppose no one else cared what my weight was, but I did. I hated the impersonal recording of my expanding girth. Then a wait until an examining room was available for a physical checkup and a consultation with the doctor. No matter how recently I had showered, I always seemed to have a hot flash and I always ended up apologizing to the doctor for greeting him sopping wet. He checked the scars, the breast, the glands, checked all over for the dreaded signs of recurrence.

And then I would produce a list of complaints. So many things were going wrong with my body near the end of treatment I could hardly believe it. Since I doubted anyone else would ever believe me, I started writing everything down and keeping records.

Here is a list I compiled before one treatment cycle under the title, "Simultaneous Discomforts":

1. Pain on the side near ribs
2. Dry eyes—cornea scratch
3. Leg and back pain—is it related to weight?
4. Three and a half weeks of almost a constant headache
5. Dizzy the last two weeks
6. Constant cold, earache and sore throat
7. Hot flashes getting worse—night flashes a big problem

One at a time, none of these ailments was too staggering. But taken together, with little relief, they were overwhelming. This is the story of chemotherapy. No dramatic smash of pain, no profuse bleeding, just an eroding of human will, nerve and energy. I often wondered if the cure was worth the fight I had to make to survive it.

We learned in our chemo group that anticancer drugs played havoc with the reproductive system. Some doctors advised their male patients to put their sperm into sperm banks. Infertility was not an infrequent side effect. If women were premenopausal, chemotherapy induced menopause and, of course, all the change-of-life symptoms, among them hot flashes and vaginal dryness.

One woman's husband had left her at the beginning of treatment, shortly after her mastectomy, and returned home after nine months. On his first night home, they tried making love, but it was a disaster. Her body was unable to manufacture any lubricants during intercourse. Their reunion was painful and highly unsatisfactory. The husband became extremely angry and she couldn't very well explain the bodily changes to him because she hardly understood them herself.

In the normal course of events, this woman would have probably been too shy to share her experiences with anyone. But within the closed little world of our chemo treatment group, we knew we were all experiencing miseries that others couldn't begin to comprehend. In the halls we spoke of private matters we wouldn't have thought of blurting out to a relative stranger, let alone do our talking in a semipublic place.

I too had my problems with the premature onset of menopause. I paid emergency visits to the gynecologist for vaginal bleeding. My insides were torn apart, unexpectedly, by lovemaking. Because of the dryness in the vagina, a normal problem because of the onset of hormonal change and menopause, heightened by horrible side effects of chemotherapy, problems and misunderstandings did occur. No one talked about it. It was taboo.

All too often comfort and advice were given shyly in the hall of the clinic outside the treatment room. Knowledge was gained from *Vogue, Time* and gossip. Finally, the nurses began to share information. It helped, for instance, to learn from one of them that Vaseline petroleum jelly was a better lubricant than K-Y jelly.

During treatment I served on a panel for chemo patients and their families with a gynecologist, and the question of lubricants came up. The doctor on this panel, which was supposed to be helping chemotherapy patients adjust, said that K-Y jelly was adequate. I begged to differ with him. I figured I knew; I had experienced what he was talking about. Other people had shared their experiences with me, and it fortified my courage to tell this man that he was not giving an adequate answer. I think I angered him, but too much was at stake for too many patients.

A few years later, I met the doctor again. He apologized for questioning me. He had recently had cancer and had gone through chemotherapy, and said he finally understood my advice because of the abuse he had endured in related areas.

The medical profession didn't seem to have a complete understanding of the problems cancer patients faced in maintaining viable, satisfactory sexual relationships. Many people wanted to withdraw from sex. Others wanted to participate in sexual activities frequently because the act reasserted life. Some doctors I met were even unable to give practical advice about sex during chemo. I felt they underestimated the real importance of keeping sexual relationships alive. At the top of the research agenda must come the delicacy of sexual relationships and sexuality itself.

The whole problem of premature menopause, lack of good information and forewarning can be illustrated with a story. A friend, a poet and writer who had been through chemo and immunology two years ahead of me, asked me with gusto one day, "Did you get your juices back yet?" I didn't know I could even expect to. It was information I hugged to myself with delight. Something to look forward to. Sometime after she had questioned me, my friend and I were seated at the head table of a meeting. I was delighted to lean over and tell her, "I've got my juices back, and I'm loving every minute of it!"

Many times during the bleak days I asked myself who would be the best person in our family to get cancer if it should happen to any of us. I decided God picked the right person. I knew I could lick it. I could handle it.

And yet, even if I felt it is better that this happened to me, the irony is, I can accept this philosophically and peacefully because, through Michael, I was finally able to experience the deep, abiding, enduring love that follows the flash of passion. There is a feeling of gratitude that I experienced this full range of joyous emotion to offset in balance the anguish of fear when faced with the real possibility of death. To have to confront early death without the precious experience of passion and deep love would really be a tragedy.

The chronicle of chemo was not only one of miseries. There were also glorious moments, times of service, creativity, merriment and pleasure.

Michael and I took Stuart on some small trips to Cape Cod, New York and Florida during these years. We consciously "made memories." We wanted to accelerate our private times and intensify our experiences. Often we would go on mini-holidays so that I could build myself up for the next round of treatment.

There were Stuart's birthday parties, which, like Cathy's and David's, always had themes and were great festive undertakings. On his ninth birthday, we took nine boys in an RV to Blossom Music Center for Serendipity Sunday. We did not skip a tradition we had started when he was five, birthday with Big Bird from "Sesame Street"; at six a live animal demonstration, with snakes, the special favorite for six boys at the Museum of Natural History; at seven, juggling and magic lessons and demonstrations for that many friends; and then at eight, kite kits for eight friends to make and fly their own kites. Each July happening was a treat.

On July 4, 1978, Michael and I sat visiting with a group of our friends, and suddenly a plan for a party was born. We would have our own harvest, an "East Side Farmers' Market Party," on the site where our old friend David had his sharecropper's garden. Three couples spent the summer planning an event that would be a knockout. We created the total atmosphere of a farmers' market with an entry arch replete with live chickens, other animals, and produce. We wore necklaces of garlic to ward off evil spirits.

Planning this party saved me. Instead of focusing on my predicament, I used energy to prepare outrageous, incredible treats for people I loved. The planning meetings for the three couples who staged the party were a lifeline. Instead of crying at home I was out shedding tears of laughter.

Also during this period WomenSpace was experiencing growing pains and financial struggles. We met every weekend to plan for the week's survival and determine how to keep the project alive. Often these meetings were held on the day after the treatment cycle. The passion for the cause of our women's coalition gave me adrenaline to fight my personal battles so that I could get out and keep the WomenSpace project alive. My survival and this goal were linked inextricably.

When all else failed, when I was really down, Michael and I went to movies. What an escape! The movie gave me a change of scene and an idea to explore. Someone often had worse problems than I did. I cried for the heroine of the movie instead of myself.

One of the things that kept me going was having something to anticipate. Sometimes what I looked forward to was a grand event. Sometimes it was small. Anticipation was indispensable in mustering up will and drive to live.

But even anticipating coming events failed finally: Eighteen months into the treatment I wanted to quit. I was tired of the nausea, vomiting, hair loss. I hated looking fat, and I hated feeling fatigued and exhausted all the time. Yes, I wanted to quit, to give up the fight. The doctors never told me I *had* to finish the protocol. We bargained with one another for me to continue for one session at a time, just one more session.

Then something occurred that put the fight back into me. A very good friend of mine died, and within a year her husband remarried. He had been lovely to her when she was ill and had given her a great deal of happiness during their brief marriage. Now someone else made love to her husband, raised her children, lived in her house and used her dishes. What an impact that remarriage had on me. From then on, whenever I was tempted to quit, I fantasized another woman lying in my bed, making love to my husband, using my things. I vowed it would never happen to me.

- *9* -

A tradition began to emerge relating to patients' last round of chemotherapy. It began when I saw a huge sheet of cake a nineteen-year-old boy brought in on his last day with the message LAST DAY OF CHEMO—LET THE SUN SHINE IN.

When my final day came, I presented the department with a human torso in chocolate saying FINISH CHEMO OR BUST. I had begun on October 10, 1977, I ended on August 10, 1979.

The funny thing was I really expected my life to change overnight. I wanted to be well right away. I assumed that the added weight would instantly melt away, leaving me with a ravishing, voluptuous, but petite, size 6 figure. My hair would come back long and flowing, thick, manageable. I would regain my former vitality and become what I was before.

It wasn't to be. My body had no way of knowing that I wasn't going to have another round of treatment immediately. A long time passed before I came to grips with the new reality that I would never be what I was before, and that I would need a lot of training to be what I wanted to become.

When the treatments ended I had a strange, unexpected reaction. I became paranoid, afraid. If the drugs weren't circulating in my system anymore, maybe I wasn't safe. Maybe there was still a cancer cell swimming free. I shared this curious reluctance to face life free of anticancer drugs with other patients. This nagging suspicion that cancer might return if aggressive chemo was not being used is sometimes called "separation syndrome." I was scared that if I wasn't doing anything to fight cancer it might come back very soon.

At the close of treatments I underwent two days of intensive testing, as I had twice before. Every six months I was checked with liver scans, bone scans, X ray, mammogram, blood tests, physicals; every part and crevice of my body was examined by human touch, by trained eyes and by the newest technology of nuclear medicine. Each time I was given the message I was "clean." We all used the word, and I did, too. But no, I hate that word. "Clean" implies I was dirty when I had cancer. I wasn't dirty. I had a disease. I was unwell. Now I prefer to use the word "well."

Speaking of words, I am on a rampage against the word "victim," in relation to cancer. I wasn't a victim of anything. I was a person, a patient, but never a victim. I have discovered that the language we use is very important because it symbolizes how we feel about ourselves and others. It affects our attitudes. With regard to cancer, the words "clean" and "victim" should be avoided.

For two years the drugs had had a chance to invade my entire system—two years of destroying good cells as well as bad. I reasoned that it would take more than a day for all of the good cells to regenerate, more than a day for all the chemical imbalances to right themselves. After all the disasters of chemotherapy, the debilitating side effects, the disruption of my life, the chaos and fear it caused in the lives of those I loved, I anticipated feeling a sense of relief and freedom when the final treatment was over. I just couldn't believe the depression I had at separation from chemo, and the quick annihilation of my expectations for a quick recovery.

But the determination to change my dreams into reality allowed me to take charge of my life once again. I had finished with sickness and I was committed to controlling a new phase: my health, my road to recovery.

After the paranoia following the treatments, I began an extensive one-woman cancer research program that led me to medical libraries and cancer research centers all around the country. There were other methods to control and destroy cancer cells. Why shouldn't I try them? What did other doctors do for their postchemotherapy patients? It seemed they did nothing. Everyone I talked to advised me to wait. Wait for what? Researchers say the experimental drugs should not be used until cancer recurs.

Well, I wasn't waiting for cancer to return. I was determined to fight for a complete recovery and an extended lifetime. No other wife would invade my private domain. With this illogical reasoning I designed a new active pattern for controlling my new life, free of disease.

-*10*-

The first thing I needed to do on the way to recovery was take off the fifty-two pounds I had gained during chemotherapy. I needed to return to a reasonable size for my pride and for my comfort.

Mrs. Eugene McCarthy once said: "I am what I am, I am who I am, I am my age." In the early fall of 1979, I said: "I am what I am, I am who I am, I am fat."

I had to accept myself realistically and decide that the size toward which I would aim would not be a measure of my success as a wife, mother or career person, but rather it would be a realistic frame for my human wholeness and an acceptable shape for my own sense of pride.

Weight loss was important to me because it had been a problem most of my life. When I was young, I wore "Chubettes." This was the name of the size dress I wore about age twelve before I went into pre-teens. The battle of sizes began then and has continued for a lifetime. Consider the humiliation of being a Chubette. You've already read my feelings about loss of control during therapy when I wore fat-lady clothes, half sizes, generous proportions for the "fuller figure." What turns of phrase! What subterfuge! When is a 6 not a 6? It's when you can't fit into any of your clothes! A close friend joked with me that I had been size 6 two times in my life, and each time I went out to buy a new wardrobe.

Size and scale became my enemies. All my anger was directed at them. For years I would not wear white pants or a white suit because white was supposed to make a person look fatter, so I avoided white and used more black. After I felt well again, I shook off that old mystique and bought myself a smashing white suit in which I felt terrific inside my skin and, I think, looked great too.

Mount Sinai Medical Center, the same institution where I underwent chemotherapy, has one of the most ambitious and well-organized programs in the country to cure obesity using supplemental fasting. The Nutrition Program, developed by Dr. Victor Vertes and Dr. Saul Genuth, was designed to treat patients who have at least fifty pounds to lose. It is estimated that there are at least 45 million people in our country who suffer from the disease of obesity. Dr. Vertes and Dr. Genuth developed a safe, supervised nutritional supplement that allowed patients to fast over long periods of time, in order to take off monumental amounts of weight.

After finishing chemotherapy in the fall of 1979, I entered the Nutrition Program again, as the patient of Dr. Irene Hazelton, the glamorous, brilliant department head. Dr. Hazelton had achieved encouraging results using behavior modification along with supplemental fasting to control obesity. I knew of her excellent work and had even interviewed her for my radio show a few years earlier.

Ironically, I saw her nearly every time I went to the hospital for chemotherapy because the Nutrition Department was located on the same floor as the Oncology Division. As I steadily gained weight during chemo, I watched Dr. Hazelton move down the corridors of the hospital, slim and confident. She became a symbol for me in those dark days of nausea and pain, a symbol of what I wanted to become, once free of cancer.

The time finally came for me to activate my plan for recovery and restoration and I made an appointment to see Dr. Hazelton. Not only was my task to lose a lot of weight, but to try and change thoroughly ingrained eating habits which had been established over a lifetime.

In the nonjudgmental atmosphere of the clinic, we learned to make friends with the scale. The scale affirmed what each patient knew about the past week's dietary successes and failures. It did not manufacture information; it merely confirmed it. I always presented myself for weigh-in garbed in something lightweight. As I looked around at my fellow dieters, I realized we all shared the same tendency to wear as little as possible at our weekly weigh-in.

The clinic staff also monitored blood pressure, pulse and actual changes in the blood. In my case, the blood test was extremely important because chemo severely depleted the disease-fighting components in my blood. A constant surveillance was necessary to make sure the diet did not adversely affect my ability to fight disease.

One of the first things I did was get rid of all the clothes in my closet that didn't fit. It was depressing going to the closet every morning, seeing reminders of a much thinner time, and knowing that there was a battle ahead of me before I ever would be able to fit into something close to those sizes again. In addition, I kept a picture of myself that I was proud of, in a highly visible place. It was a reminder to me and others of how I really saw myself. I maintained high standards of grooming and was constantly on the lookout for cosmetics that accentuated my good, *thin* features. One of my personal vanities is pride in my thin ankles, so I indulged my love of fine hosiery as a reward.

We learned to program time for the self as an incentive for good diet behavior. If I met a particular goal, I promised myself the time to see a movie, watch a special on TV, start a novel not required for an interview or buy new clothes.

As the Thursday appointments continued, I began to lose weight consistently. My self-esteem blossomed again as I grew thinner. It was immensely satisfying to watch the pounds drop away, especially when I remembered the thoughtless people who had asked me when I was fat from the treatment for cancer, "Are you pregnant?" I secretly hated those people who mistook my fight for survival for a joyous life-giving experience. Being asked if I was pregnant on numerous occasions was one of the most cruel, depressing events of chemo.

Dr. Hazelton added a new dimension to the battle of my bulge: exercise. What a joke that was. I could hardly move, my energy supplies were so depleted. The day this new aspect of my physical fitness began, my husband photographed me in all the glory of my recently purchased walking gear, and then literally carried me to the corner and back. I began regular exercise with my neighborhood walking group, thereby getting both exercise and good gossip.

The walking wasn't confined only to familiar neighborhood paths. Michael and I walked in London, on a wonderful holiday to celebrate my forty-fifth birthday. Then we flew to Israel for my first visit to Jerusalem since my father's sudden death four months before my mastectomy. Here we made a special personal pilgrimage to my father's grave on the Mount of Olives across from the Dome of the Rock. Finally, Michael and I walked for hours in Paris. We started our meanderings from the four-teenth-century abbey where we stayed on the Left Bank, and roamed the city. This final excursion in Paris became a second honeymoon, a renewal of our love affair.

When I look back on the whole period of chemotherapy, and the intense desire I had to take control of my life after the nightmare ended, one event stands out clearly in my mind as the formal demarcation of the end of chemo memories and the beginning of a new adventure in living. Although I had been free of cancer for a short period of time and had actively participated in staying well by attacking my weight problem, I still carried painful memories around with me of the chemo experience. The event that symbolized the end and the new beginning was, of course, a party.

A few days after our return from Europe, my family-of-choice gave me a black-tie, surprise birthday breakfast at Beachwood Place, a swanky new suburban mall. The mall contained open walkways through a huge atrium, fabulous shops, fountains and a glass-enclosed elevator. What a thrill it was to return to town and see friends for the first time since our return dressed smashingly in tuxedoes and formal gowns at 7:00 in the morning.

My friends were aware of what an early riser I was, since I spoke with many of them each morning between 7:00 and 8:00. This was my prime time. The party givers presented me with an "understated" corsage of seven large, purple orchids. We dined on "Eggs Rena-Dict," drank champagne and watched a song-and-dance radio broadcast show. My first employer in the radio field and my friends produced and starred in the production.

Then, I happened to glance up and I saw many of my friends glide down the escalator, each one wearing a vintage dress or gown of mine that I had long since stored away in the attic. It's a good thing I keep my drawers in order and my attic clean.

While Michael and I were away on our trip to Europe and Israel, close friends from our family-of-choice who knew of my penchant for saving everything went into the attic to select the clothes for the incredible fashion show. As I saw the party dresses, teamed with wild hats from outfits I used for speeches, accessorized with everything from toilet plungers to tennis rackets and capped off in one instance with galoshes, I rolled with laughter.

The narrator of this lifetime fashion show was Eleanor Brenner, my designer friend from New York. By the end of the show most of us were in tears from constant laughing. The laughter was therapeutic and energizing. Somehow, the outrageous celebration and style show washed away the last of the chemo cobwebs and really did signal yet another watershed in my life.

But I never missed that special Thursday afternoon clinic time that I had carved out for myself. As I continued to shed the unwanted pounds and feel the resurgence of energy, and pride, I picked up the threads of my life, held in abeyance by the cancer and chemo. That few hours a week was my time for myself, a time when I could view the visible gratifying results of my body's gradual restoration.

- *11* -

By December 1979 I had finished chemo and, after only three months, had lost a large portion of the weight I had gained. I was feeling terrific, confident that life was on the upswing. But then, in the midst of the holiday season, a shattering loss occurred once again.

David Blaushild, who himself had survived an attack of cancer, had been one of my cheerleaders during chemotherapy and was a pivotal member of my extended family-of-choice. Throughout chemo he had constantly bullied me into living. I set out to visit David in the hospital, where he had just gone for relatively minor surgery. I was carrying a fancy shopping bag filled with outrageous get-well gifts. This was small payment because David, who looked not unlike a jolly Buddha himself, had given me the Bali sculpture that had meant so much to me after my mastectomy.

As I swung down the hall toward his room that fateful day, a nurse interrupted my progress and asked me who I was and who I was visiting. After I answered her questions, she directed me into her office. Intuitively, I knew something was wrong; I almost didn't need to be told the dreadful facts. David had died an hour before of a massive embolism, a complication resulting from his surgery.

What a nightmare!

I had just talked to David two days earlier, right before his surgery. He was vibrant and full of jokes, pranks and plans. I suddenly realized that my dear friend Marilyn Blaushild was left a widow for the second time in her forty-eight years. I imagined how painful and difficult the funeral arrangements were going to be when children and an ex-wife would gather to mourn.

In that instant I knew an era in our life had ended. For Michael, it was the loss of a kindred spirit, his foil, his friend. For Stuart, it was losing a grandfather all over again. For me, it was like losing a brother. David understood as no one else did my outrageous thrust of extracting the most out of each moment. He freed me by conspiring to find every crack in my exterior to permit the best to come through. Life would go on, but never in the same way.

This event triggered an awesome, awful, inexplicable pain in me. In life, David had forced me to concentrate on survival. Through his death, he forced me to face an even greater issue: my own mortality.

The first Thursday of 1980 began much like any other day. As I got into the car to drive to the hospital for my weekly nutrition clinic appointment, I remember feeling good because I had lost nearly thirty pounds and was beginning to feel trim. I looked forward to the ritual confirmation from my old nemesis and new friend, the clinic scale. As I opened the car door and stepped onto the hospital parking lot surface, a sudden, swift shock of pain flashed through me, a pain so severe, it stopped me cold. I couldn't quite believe the enormous amount of pain I was experiencing. I sat back down on the seat of the car, thinking that if I kept still for a moment, the pain would disappear. It was a vain hope. Each time I moved out of the car, the searing, white-hot pain stabbed through my body. My legs seemed unable to support my weight. The intensity of the pain was that debilitating.

I kept making deals with myself and with the pain. If I could inch myself to the hospital door without feeling the riveting pain, then I would allow that pain to return once I was safely ensconced in the clinic's waiting room. But my body wasn't listening to any deals. As I moved slowly toward the door, the pain jarred me every few seconds. The goal of reaching the clinic assumed Herculean proportions.

Finally, I made it to a chair in the cool blue of the clinic's reception area. I had to marshal my strength to get up and fill out the weekly "check-in sheet report card" that is part of the clinic's ritual. After completing the form, I sank once again into the safe haven of the chair and began to cry. The tears ran through my mascaraed lashes, making dirty little rivuletlike marks on my once impeccably made up face. How unutterably long ago it seemed that I had stood in front of the bathroom mirror and made up my face. Was it only that morning?

I kept asking myself over and over, as I sat weeping, Why me? Why now? Why this new gut-wrenching pain?

I thought I was finished with agony. How much more could my body endure? How much more could I endure?

I looked up and through my tears I watched Dr. Hazelton approach. She took in my extreme distress in one comprehensive empathetic glance, and gently guided me into her office.

"What's wrong?" she asked me.

"I don't know," I replied. "I really don't know."

She asked me to describe what I was feeling. I told her about the sudden inexplicable onset of tremendous pain, and I shared with her my feelings of panic because the pain was so excruciating. She softly explained that similar reactions occur in many patients who have been fighting chronic illnesses. People tend to hold their emotions in check in order to save their psychological strength for the big fight. Emotions rigidly suppressed break through the stringently imposed control. Fighting so hard to survive and, in my case, fighting to survive the cure, too, causes patients never to face the big issue. What

I was experiencing at that moment, and what many other people have experienced, was a delayed reaction for not facing the huge, underlying problem. I was having a delayed reaction to not confronting the issue of my own mortality.

I had thought about death in an abstract way. I had fantasized my own funeral, crowded, packed with friends. I had wondered who would come, who would care. I had even left verbal and written instructions! Just bury me in a simple, unadorned, white pine box, and, romantically, place one bird-of-paradise flower on it to symbolize my colorful life. Don't spend a lot on the coffin and the flowers. I had thought about the scenario, but I had never faced the reality.

I understood what Dr. Hazelton was saying. I recognized dimly that I hadn't taken out those deeply buried feelings, thoughts and ideas and examined them. And I guess I even understood why I, and thousands like me, couldn't. When anyone is intimately involved with a struggle for her or his survival, confronting the hard issue of death seems a rather self-defeating, even inappropriate, activity. So the notion and all the emotional dressing are shelved for the while, to be taken out and thoroughly inspected at a less intense time. What I couldn't understand was why I had such a terrific reaction to my delayed emotional bookkeeping in this of all places, this one place that had been, in the months during chemo and after, such a shining oasis of help and well-being.

Dr. Hazelton asked me to explore the events of recent weeks and search out the trauma that had forced me to release those powerful emotions dammed up for such a long time. And then, of course, it was obvious. David. His death only two weeks before triggered the awesome reality. Somehow, my body had waited until I arrived at the hospital to send forth its message.

Dr. Hazelton's main concern, however, on that bewildering,

blustery January day wasn't urging me to examine my notions about my own death, but to relieve the paralyzing pain that had resulted from my emotional flashback and confrontation. There was time enough for analyzing the deeper problems later. Right then, the priority was to get rid of the pain. She asked me if I wanted to try something unusual that might relieve the pain. I desperately needed to feel some relief and was willing to try anything.

Dr. Hazelton told me to draw an imaginary circle around my body, encompassing the total body mass. At her low-keyed suggestion, I drew the circle again and again, to make sure that my body was totally enclosed in the imaginary border. Then she told me to place a wedge where the pain was, and break the circle. I drove a wedge, which looked in my mind's eye like the kind of stopper put under a door to prevent it from sliding, into the circle, in the direction of the pain. To my utter and complete amazement, the pain eased immediately. I repeated the exercise once more at Dr. Hazelton's recommendation. The pain disappeared. I just sat quietly for a moment, filled with a sense of incredulous wonder.

This was my first introduction to hypnotherapy, and I was seduced. If a directly induced trancelike state could eliminate such powerful pain, training the mind to obey certain commands could work in other areas of my life, too. It seemed to me that hypnotherapy could become a powerful weapon in organizing my body's immune responses against another invasion of cancer. Here was the best preventive medicine I had discovered yet. Hypnotherapy could help me ward off the possible return of disease and eliminate for me, perhaps, the necessity of ever having to participate again in the nightmare that is chemo.

Not only did I break the circle of pain, but I established a new relationship with Dr. Hazelton and took one more positive step toward controlling my health—and my life. Of course, that terrifying, debilitating pain was the signal that told me what issue I first wanted to confront during hypnotherapy. I had to look the fact of my own death straight in the eye. I really didn't want any woman replacing me in the overall scheme of things. I didn't want someone else taking my place with my husband, or making decisions about raising my children. I wanted to live.

- *12* -

My new routine, my hypnotherapy sessions, were held with Dr. Hazelton in another locale, The Saltzman Institute for Clinical Investigation. The quietness of the waiting area the first day made me feel uneasy, but then Dr. Hazelton appeared and ushered me to her office, the "safe place." What a peaceful, quiet area this new space was. The room itself was tiny and rectangular. On the right, upon entering, was a flat, dark brown sofa that reminded me of the stereotypical Freudian couch. On the left sat a straight-backed beige, upholstered chair, and beyond that, a large leather important-looking chair and ottoman. No windows relieved the starkness of the walls, only a few pictures. There was one lamp in the room and a box of tissues on a narrow wooden table. The dimness, the simplicity, wrapped me in a cocoon of safety.

The choice of chair itself became an exercise and a message. My preferences changed according to my mood and need. At first, I sat rigid and upright on the straight chair. Later, during a session, I would change my seat because of a change in mood or emphasis. I did what felt right. Dr. Hazelton and I entered into a special partnership. She brought her skills as a sensitive physician and therapist to the relationship; I brought my desire, will and imagination.

The few days every six months before checkups for recurrence of cancer are a continuing source of tremendous stress. I call the symptoms of the stress the checkup crazies. It is a rational anxiety and is easily recognizable. It is a strange, recurring, common malady for anyone who has confronted major illness. The symptoms include waking up at 3:00 or 4:00 A.M. often with nightmares, shortness of breath, binging on food (or not eating at all), fatigue, loss of temper, occasionally diarrhea and usually teariness at unexpected moments. My symptoms also include more frenzied activities such as obsessive closet cleaning. This group of symptoms are readily recognized by those who have experienced them; it is the fear that tomorrow you may have a bad diagnosis.

Basically, understanding the problem is the key to treating it and reinstating balance. At the time of subsequent checkups or doctor's visits, people with chronic disease experience the same trauma they had at the original discovery of the illness. The response to that memory causes extreme anxiety, and it must be dealt with and neutralized.

I have checkups every six months, or more frequently if I observe a frightening body change, and I almost always have a case of "checkup crazies." However, with Dr. Hazelton's help, I have learned some positive ways to deal with my anxiety.

First, I schedule my doctor's appointment at a time far in advance so that I can allow for several hours at the hospital in case a test is late or needs to be repeated. I get hold of a good book and save it for the waiting hours. This way I use the time for my own pleasure and also divert my attention from all the patients around me in the testing area, who are replete with IVs, drainage bags and signs of physical deterioration. Since I know I identify with them and get fearful, I preplan my protection and diversion.

I have found it helps to make a point of talking to the people who are testing me. Somehow, this contact lessens the impersonality of the tests and infuses this cold situation with humanity, and reduces stress. If I am having a bone or liver

85

scan which are particularly frightening to me, I use meditation or trance, learned in hypnotherapy, to relax myself. A touch of trance, being transported to a safe, comfortable, optimistic place in my consciousness, brings relaxation and the reduction of my raw fear.

I also try to have my work organized and finished well ahead of time. I tape extra radio programs and schedule other activities so that I can make the two days of testing a miniholiday. If I find I am not as patient and tolerant at home or at the office, I joke and honestly apologize by saying the truth: "I'm having the 'checkup crazies.' "

I am extremely lucky to have doctors who are kind and considerate and call me at the end of the day's testing with the results. If you know your physician well, you can phone him and let him know this is your testing period and you would like your results as soon as possible. By alerting him you will help single yourself out from his patient load, and he will make an effort to get you your results quickly. Each day you wait for the results is almost always another night's sleep lost. Not only will it make you "crazy," it can also affect your health. Calling ahead and getting information as quickly as possible is a large part of making a plan for your improved personal protection.

The "checkup crazies" are almost impossible to avoid if you are afflicted with chronic disease. But acknowledging that you are afraid and making strides toward dealing with the anxiety go a long way toward conquering them. For me, my work with Dr. Hazelton—learning to relax, meditate and refresh myself through trance—also contributed to my ability to deal with this problem.

The more Dr. Hazelton and I talked about the amorphous thing called death, the more I realized it wasn't the loss of life I feared, but the loss of control over my life. I didn't want approaching death to disfigure me. I had always been the one who directed the show. Approaching death might wrest that responsibility from my hands and the finale would be a failure. Some of my feelings were symbolized in my preoccupation with my appearance, but even those feelings stemmed from an all-pervasive fear that I would eventually lose control. And those newly won feelings of pride in being able to stay in control, of having some power over my destiny, I cherished.

I didn't relish fantasies of my imminent death or the approach of death itself destroying everything I fought long and hard for. I didn't want to disintegrate bit by bit in an undignified way. I didn't want to be ugly. No way did I want anyone seeing me with my roots exposed and my body full of tubes and bags. I worried about being a financial drain. I trembled at the thought of my mind and mouth rambling because I was pumped full of pain-killing, mind-distorting drugs. Over the years I had seen a few close friends go through everything I've described. I vowed, not me! I would fight for dignity and control and I would end my own life at the right time.

Ironically, we all worry that at the "right time" we might be unable to do it, to or for ourselves. So as Dr. Hazelton and I talked, I emptied out all the horrors. Then a question came so quickly, so directly, that after I uttered it I was spent: Is there some way to control pain? I wanted to know if there is some way to close down the body when peace is longed for and all is in order with special human relationships.

After I had shaped the question that emerged from some buried layer of consciousness, then and only then did Dr. Hazelton begin to speak to the deep place. She told me it was possible to control pain. Yes, I could, in fact, close down my body when I chose.

She told me about Hospice, a new community service that helps a person at home or in a special hospital with a homelike setting. Hospice is both a place and a program to turn to when

87

curing is no longer possible and gentle supportive caring is the objective.

I learned about Brompton Mixture, or Hospice Mix, a liquid a person can drink to take the edge off the horrendous pain, yet still stay at the edge of consciousness to be aware and able to communicate. Since Brompton Mix can be had on demand, the necessity of waiting for a nurse to come and give a shot to stop pain is eliminated. The patient has the dignity and the security of control sitting on the table right next to the bed.

She told me of partnerships. She explained how in Hospice caring persons stay with a patient until just before the end.

But it was the hypnotherapy that proved totally unlike any perception related to psychiatry or hypnosis I had ever had. Hypnotherapy was direct and honest. The thrill I discovered was that this was a forward-moving process. The past was respected, used sparingly where vignettes could give a lead for healing, but there was no guilt here. It was an impartial, nonjudgmental process whose sole aim seemed to be to help the inquirer move forward soundly and steadily.

Hypnotherapy was, as author-practitioner Milton Erickson once said when describing the process, "Two people get together and one tries to help the other figure out what he wants."

I probed for information from many levels of my mind. I dug into my soul and then Dr. Hazelton organized cues I gave her. She spoke to the portion of the mind I revealed. I was ready to focus totally and receive the information she offered.

When I heard about possibilities of personal control, when Dr. Hazelton told me she had actually been with people literally up to one hour before they chose to die, in their time, in their way, I felt as if a huge weight were removed from my being. I had always visualized death as a long tunnel with lights at the end. Along the journey through the tunnel, shadowy silhouettes of loved ones would reach out to touch and say good-bye. She told me she had heard about similar imagery from her patients.

I felt teary. I felt light. I was happy. I was exhausted. I wanted to fly and dance down the hall. I was energized. We dealt with death at last.

Death is a real, personal issue, especially when dealing with one's own. Confronting one's own death is not a time to hold the subject at arm's length. It is threatening, but it must be faced.

What I am expressing applies not only to persons who have had cancer. Coronary patients or any others with chronic life-threatening diseases get frightened when they hear of an untimely death. And, of course, all death is untimely for those who would want to see the dawn one more day. A man is frightened when he hears that a colleague has dropped dead in his forties or fifties . . . or sixties or seventies. He vows to reduce his stress, slow down the rat race, eat more sensibly, relax his pace, exercise. In a flash a whole survival regimen is designed, activated instantly, and forgotten ten days after the funeral and first mourning period are over. This is a natural response because it is the precious healing from the tincture of time that lets us not walk around wounded, but allows us to bind up our wounds and fight the raw pain—often in the presence of seeming madness and inequity—find balance and continue living.

One humorous side effect of the shock of death is that wives will become solicitous, gentle, warm, loving, exceptionally kind to a husband to compensate for feelings of fear and even guilt when hearing of the death of a friend's husband. I do it; others I know have confessed they do too. We laugh and acknowledge it and ease off to our more normal relationship, as the sting of death recedes.

Through the changing of seasons, nature reminds us, and warns us, about the inherent mysteries of life, the measured patterns of beauty. For people who live in a warmer climate with limited variations all year long, the message is not as sharp and dramatic. But as I look out of the glass doors in our garden room, over our rolling backyard, and see a panorama of changes from crocuses and emperor tulips, to day lilies, roses and raspberries, to mums and, finally, to multicolored fall leaves, I am reminded vividly of cycles and my place in the universe.

I hope I do not die in the spring and be denied the promise of the seasons. Perhaps I know inside I will die in the fall because of my new capabilities in self-hypnosis. I will return to the earth in the fall and rest with leaves and then snow blanketing me.

Part Two

Celebrations:
New Patterns
for Living

What's really important is life as a celebration.

—Abraham Joshua Heschel
in an interview withCarl Stern

INTRODUCTION

One of the first things a person does when granted an extra measure of life after either a severe illness or a frightening brush with death is to make a crashing reappraisal of what they actually do with their life. They check out the status of their relationships, they review their use of time with regard to both work and play; in short, they assess their patterns for living.

Most people change or modify some aspect of their lives. Actually, healthy people should pretend for a moment that a disaster might occur and force themselves to do this crucial personal appraisal and assessment. Well or recovering, it is always in order to create new patterns for living.

Any brush with death heightens a person's awareness and forces that person to appreciate things often taken for granted. It's beyond comprehension how a fight for survival wouldn't reawaken the survivor to the beauty of the world and the worth of the people in it.

But I prefer to look at a life-threatening experience in a different way. Cancer conquerors already had some appreciation of life before they got the disease. They were contributors, challengers, "excited about the future," as Norman Cousins says, not because they feared death, but because they fully intended living to a ripe, fruitful old age. If they feared anything, it was that the ravages of disease might cause them to lose control and prevent them from participating fully in mainstream activities. Cousins continually hammers home, in both *Human*

Options and *An Anatomy of an Illness,* that purpose, creativity and the will to live considerably enhance longevity.

Before anyone enters the battle against a debilitating, life-threatening disease, those qualities ought to be thoroughly ingrained personality traits. Mine were. My parents set an example by how they each lived after they both had coronaries. I modeled my behavior after theirs, incorporating their patterns for coping into my life.

Optimism and involvement in the arena beyond self are the best life insurance policies known to us. The willingness to embrace life, to improve the quality of living is the ultimate gratification.

When I look back I see not only how the battle against cancer changed me, but the positive qualities I carried with me into the fight. My participation in the women's movement, for example, was involvement in a life-giving revolution. It is my feeling that the final goal of feminism is not simply the liberation of women, but the freeing of men and children as well. My dedication to the reclamation of Playhouse Square and other projects in my community was life-giving, too. The revitalization of a once-elegant urban area restores the whole community. Finally, there was my determination to nurture personal relationships, taking care of the most basic life-giving forces there are.

While I was reviewing my battles, I came across photocopied pages from an old desk diary. The pages detail my life in May 1978, a month during which I had chemo treatments. I had marked big, black *C*'s on the five days indicating treatments. I have to admit not too much else was scheduled for those days. But the rest of the days of the month were barely readable, telling me that as I struggled with the side effects from the anticancer drugs, and fought for my life, I didn't operate at peak efficiency, but I never gave up.

As I examine the past, I see distinct phases. There was a

brief period of singlehood, followed by marriage and mothering, then the volunteering that I added in my discretionary free time, and finally my emergence into the world of work.

Then came my involvement in the women's movement, which I view as a natural blending of public and private commitments. Next came the fight against cancer and, finally, in a stubborn determination to control my body and to prevent a recurrence of cancer, the practice of hypnotherapy.

During each phase, I stockpiled ideas and gathered useful tools, always rearranging priorities, constantly juggling the disparate parts of the whole. From this gigantic experiential education, I designed what I've come to call "patterns for headstrong living."

The patterns are flexible and can be altered to apply toward any future crises or experiences. Because these patterns have worked so well for me, I want to share them. Some are probably incorporated in the daily fabric of your life already. Some could suggest better ways to cope with the stresses of living, but all of these patterns enhance a conquering, celebrating, headstrong life.

INTIMATE RELATIONSHIPS

Women seem to need and are perhaps psychologically and biologically inclined to form strong attachments with other human beings. Relationships with partners, children, and other family members, as well as special friends are of paramount importance.

From childhood on we learn from our intimate relationships. We bounce new ideas off other people who are important to us. Our development can be measured through the development of the other. The special person reflects our images of ourselves. Within a small circle of important people we learn to nurture and to accept nurturing in return.

Very often, it seems to me, men invest their most intimate selves only in a serious relationship with a woman. Their friendships with other men are active, yet formed mostly for comradeship, not for the purpose of exchanging confidences. While they may sometimes deplore the nature of women's friendships with other women, men seem to secretly envy a woman's ability to share intimate thoughts, particularly with another woman. They view this sharing as a source of strength for women. What a relief to be able to unburden yourself to a nonjudgmental, caring other. Sadly, men are rarely taught to do this.

Never is the need for strong, close attachments more apparent than when a person faces a great crisis. During that time the inclination is to present a normal front to most of the world.

If we can carry on as usual, we feel we are preserving a certain measure of dignity and also a certain amount of personal control. I found this to be true as I fought through the two years of chemotherapy. Most of the women in my chemo group only let themselves go with a few special chosen people. Those people may have been spouses or a close friend. One woman said she couldn't have worked through the fears without the constant support of her husband. She also told us he helped her considerably by easing the practical concerns of day-to-day living that assume gigantic proportions when one is taking anticancer drugs.

In my case I depended on a few close women friends. When I really needed to talk, to share my fears and my enormous pain, I knew I could call on them.

My friend Addrianne had had a mastectomy and gone through two years of chemotherapy one year before I did. She knew from personal experience what I was facing. The day before I began each treatment cycle she called me from England so that I could unburden myself and she could commiserate and encourage. Those calls didn't lessen the physical ravages of the drugs, but they certainly helped me face more positively what was to come.

The women in my extended family-of-choice allowed me to pour out all the fears and pain I was experiencing that I wouldn't or couldn't express to anyone else. They forced me to see that it wasn't weakness to accept help from my friends. They seemed to know I needed a prod to ask for help. And without the help I did have to ask for, I couldn't have got through those two years. When I was ready to give up, to stop taking the chemo drugs, they were the people who urged me to continue. Without their constant concern and support, I might have discontinued the life-giving, torturous treatments.

Everyone needs a few intimate relationships, be they with a friend, lover or spouse. These special relationships should be carefully developed and nurtured over the years, but if they have not been, it is never too late to reach out. Don't be afraid to call on them in times of crisis or in times of joy.

APPEARANCE

Appearance is the barometer of how we feel about ourselves and a measure of how well we take care of our bodies. What we eat, what we wear, what kinds of medicines we take, the amount of exercise we get are all part of how we look.

Never is taking care of our bodies more important than when suffering from chronic disease. The seemingly self-indulgent things like worrying about what we wear and the cosmetics we use are important details to pay attention to when ill. A relaxing bubble bath can help relieve the fatigue and psychological pressures that are associated with a critical illness. Wearing bright comfortable clothes can lift the spirits.

Good nutrition habits are especially important when sick. Even though food often doesn't taste good, a well-balanced diet is necessary to maintain the body strength to fight the disease. Families can help out by experimenting with different types of nutritionally sound recipes that also tempt the appetite.

Although vigorous exercise is about the furthest thing from a chronically ill person's mind, a short walk can provide a change of scene, reduce stress and help induce a pleasant tiredness instead of the enervating fatigue most chronically ill people experience.

Everyone should be careful about the medicine she or he takes and the manner in which it is prescribed. I feel strongly that no one should smoke and every one of us should use alcohol in moderation.

When I underwent chemotherapy, concern for my appearance

helped me feel better about myself, and there were specific things I did in regard to my appearance to help reduce the stress related to the body destruction the chemo drugs caused. When I gained so much weight during chemo, I wore bright colors and a flower at my neckline so that people would notice my face and not my swollen belly. I turned my bathroom into a mini-spa and experimented with different kinds of cosmetics and moisturizers in order to combat the drying effects of the drugs.

I have found that the better cancer patients take care of their bodies, the brighter the colors they wear, the better they eat, the better able they are to cope with the ravages of the disease and the debilitating side effects of the cure.

A word about breast reconstruction surgery: Many women, after having a mastectomy, consider reconstructive surgery to restore the breast. If a woman is uncomfortable with or dissatisfied with a particular body part, the dissatisfaction and discomfort generally spill over into other areas of her life. The art of reconstructive surgery is so advanced there is no reason not to take advantage of the skills the science offers if you have the money and the need to do so.

PRIVATE TIME

Every person needs time alone. Private time is necessary for thinking about goals and priorities. We need to have time to plan, to reassess values, and simply to daydream and fantasize. Time away from the pressures of family and society is reviving and energizing. Like everything else in a busy life, time alone has to be scheduled and demanded without guilt.

Finding time to be by myself was one of the things I learned to do only after I had developed cancer. I believe also that if I had been in the habit of finding a few private moments each day for myself, I could have dealt with much of the stress that I had accumulated throughout my life. I can't help thinking that I might have even prevented the cancer if I had learned years ago to enjoy being by myself and reflect on the traumas and pain that were, at times, a part of my life.

It doesn't matter when the private moments are found; the important thing is to take them. Some women program alone time with another activity. I have a friend who claims she does her best thinking when she jogs. Other women combine quiet time with a relaxing soak in the tub. Others say they can think better when their hands are occupied with needlework, knitting or painting.

In this fast-paced electronic age, many of us are uncomfortable with the notion of being alone. We seem to need constant stimulation. But we can't renew our minds while being bombarded by externals.

If we practice being alone, if we learn to enjoy our aloneness, feel comfortable with it, then when traumatic events occur, we are better able to confront them and deal with the stress. The concept of private time and aloneness must be converted from a negative fraught with fear and guilt to a positive that is sought after, relished, planned for and, above all, thoroughly enjoyed.

RELIGION

Death is difficult to face. For anyone fighting a chronic disease, the notion of confronting one's own mortality eventually becomes necessary in order to face the future with any kind of equanimity. The only way I can imagine dealing with death is through a developed, internalized belief system. For me, my Jewish faith and heritage has always played a very important part in my life. In an effort to face the fear that I might die, I called upon years of ritual and practice.

My sense of religion and reality are best expressed in the changes I made in a prayer recited on Yom Kippur. The prayer questions:

Who shall live?
Who shall die?

The traditional response:

. . . and repentance, prayer, and good deeds avert the severe decree.

Then in my mind I added:

Yes, and surgery and chemotherapy and radiation help avert the severe decree.
Yes, and tenacity and obstinacy and inner strength help avert the severe decree.

My survival, I felt, depended on God being a part of me. Since I believe I was created in God's image and I have seen the image manifested in others and in nature, it seems to me that it became my responsibility to maintain the spark of life I saw reflected in me and mirrored all around.

I believe also that the people who, as Dylan Thomas said, "do not go gentle into that good night," who take responsibility for mental and physical health, who fight to achieve quality daily survival, are not afraid to face death. These people have taken the time and energy to construct a belief system for actively living and surviving every phase of the life cycle.

Because of the strong religious background already established in my family, I came to my illness well equipped with deep beliefs. Not everyone is so lucky. My religious convictions were a strong source of strength to me, and I urge everyone to revitalize their own religious resources to aid in the battle.

MANAGING TIME

Managing time demands an acute awareness of goals and priorities. Everyone must juggle various roles, but the moment illness intrudes in one's life, the juggling becomes more difficult and the management of one's time more important.

I happen to be blessed with lots of energy and a well-honed ability to organize. I'm compulsive and if a person is as driven as I am, she has naturally acquired tricks of managing time somewhere along the way in order to fit twenty-six hours into a twenty-four-hour day!

In the course of my public-speaking activities, I have developed a questionnaire dealing with time management. I want to share some of the questions in the hope that the answers will suggest better ways to use and control your time.

1. Am I really in control of my time? Are my actions determined by me, not by circumstances or other people's priorities?
2. Do I have in writing a clearly defined set of lifetime goals appropriate for me?
3. Do I have a similar set of goals detailed for the next six months?
4. Do I know my physical and mental prime times?
5. Do I schedule my priority tasks during my prime time?
6. Do I delegate as much work as possible?
7. Do I delegate authority along with the responsibility?
8. Am I punctual?

9. Do I force myself to take time to plan?
10. Do I keep a personal log to determine where my time is spent?
11. Do I keep in mind the dollar value of my time?
12. Do I program nonthinking activities with thought-provoking activities?
13. Do I have time to appreciate the beauty of a rose?

During illness, managing time takes on new urgency. One is more fatigued and often in pain. Thus, daily tasks must be organized to take these facts into account. The profound problem of the possible shortening of life, itself, must also be considered at some point.

During a period of crucial illness, outside help in managing time might be necessary. One's family, one's employer, one's friends might have to be called on to help. Don't be afraid to ask.

MANAGING
STRESS

I have come to believe that a major cause of disease is the inability to control stress.

For years my coping mechanism when dealt a painful blow was to repress the hurt or anger I felt and rush headlong into another activity. I never took the time to *deal* with the stress after rejection by my first husband, the terrible scarring caused by the automobile accident or my father's death. I never allowed myself to examine what each event meant to me and I never gave myself the chance to grieve.

It was frightening for me, as I talked to the women in my chemo group, to learn that they had experienced similar traumas and reacted in much the same way. One woman had just gone through a divorce and then learned she had cancer; another had been in a terrible car accident shortly before her cancer was discovered.

The pattern began to come clear to me. Stress and the inability to confront it may have contributed to our diseases.

When I tried to sublimate another painful experience, my friend David's death, I learned how important it can be to face a stressful occurrence squarely. Fortunately, I was under the supervision of Dr. Irene Hazelton and found hypnotherapy, which has been my greatest resource for dealing with stress in a constructive manner.

I have chosen hypnotherapy to help me control stress, but there are other methods. Some people depend on exercise.

Others combine exercise and meditation. Still others have learned to be creative with anger. Many women have found assertiveness training an effective way to control stress.

The important thing is to acknowledge that certain life events are stressful, face them, and deal with them in a suitable way. If stress is denied and buried, a terrific amount of energy is lost. Also, it is thought now that a stress overload can create a drop in physical immunity levels. We all need energy, strength and vitality to maintain a healthy, active, productive life.

I would like to share some of the techniques I learned during hypnotherapy that helped me to activate my body's immune system to be constantly on the lookout for one, new and tiny microscopic cancer cell. I would also like to tell you some of the coping strategies I developed in order to deal with life's continuing destructive forces. By eliminating or at least controlling the stress accumulated in the everyday process of living, the body is freed up to deal with the urgent task of quality survival, and the mind is free to explore new avenues of growth.

Much of the basis of my work with hypnotherapy involved the use of imagery. I let my mind create an image, and through trance I set that image to work in whatever area I might be concentrating on. Because I was convinced that the body's immune system somehow fails when cancer begins its pernicious take-over, and because I believe that stress can divert precious energy away from the work of the immune system, Dr. Hazelton and I outlined these areas as our main concerns.

The idea of releasing a force to activate a surveillance mechanism and to stimulate the white cells to mobilize seemed sensible when I related it to physiology lessons I had in college. I remembered that adrenaline is released when one is frightened, and people are quickly able to fight or flee depending upon the circumstances. It was reasonable to believe that since the mind released such a powerful force in this instance, mobilizing red and white cells should be relatively easy. In addition, using the powers of the mind in this way was safe.

I had an opportunity to have lunch with writer Norman Cousins and later that same day interviewed him on the ideas in his book *Anatomy of an Illness*. That day changed my life. He autographed my book "To Rena, who has the courage of my convictions." We both lived and believed what he wrote. In our deep human exchange of ideas, we affirmed each other. That's when I resolved that my state of health could be triggered and sustained by my mind.

Dr. Hazelton first helped me develop exercises to set up a mechanism for surveillance, activated consciously by my mind, that would scan and monitor my body. For some reason, I had difficulty dealing with the word "surveillance." I couldn't pronounce it. I stumbled on it. So I created an image by breaking the word down into its three syllables. The first became "Sir," a knight. The second, "Vay" from "oy vay." The third, "Lance," the knight's spear. The image was one of a knight riding full tilt into battle, weapon raised, totally prepared to fight for my honor and my life. The knight pokes and prods white cells into action in every inch of my body. My knight even had a plume on his helmet and the color of his plume changed daily, according to what I needed "Sir-Vay-Lance" to do and be for me. The color of his plume changed chameleonlike and reflected either my mood or my surroundings. When I needed him to be especially strong and forceful, the plume was red. Sometimes I pulled myself up regally, proclaimed to myself that my survival did matter and the plume became royal purple. There were times I activated the surveillance device in my backyard and the plume changed to green. Color was also a symbol and helped me with self-awareness and total body monitoring.

I do this surveillance once a day—sometimes more frequently. Often I do it when I awake and gently activate my entire system, in a few delicate, private early morning moments. I generally also thank God for granting me another day. I ask for no favors; I don't plea-bargain. The sounds of silence are maintained while I utter a traditional Jewish prayer, *Shehecheyanu*, a prayer usually recited on holidays and special events.

> *Blessed art Thou, O Lord our God*
> *King of the Universe*
> *Who has kept us in Life,*
> *Sustained us,*
> *And enabled us to reach this day.*

And I live each day freely and completely as a holiday because my day has begun with a prayer of thanksgiving. Sir-Vay-Lance is the partner in the daily exercise of monitoring, activating the immune mechanism and alerting the surveillance system that enables me to live yet another holy holiday and protect my life.

The other surveillance technique I employ is to directly visualize strong, evocative words, like STRONG, WELL, WONDERFUL, FIGHT, LIVE. I see them in neon. I see them in capital letters. The word I pick characterizes my mood that day. If I'm feeling particularly well, the word reflects it; if I am feeling down, the words are a charge, a summons to get working on what I really want to be.

All kinds of events cause stress, but in the kind of life I lead, a life where I interact with so many different kinds of people daily, the things people say and do often cause stress.

Here are some exercises I use to lessen my humiliation and personal pain at someone's thoughtless remark, unwarranted criticism or inconsiderate deed.

First, I use an imaginary shield, a large body-size Lucite sheet. When someone is hurting me, and I can feel my body responding physically to what the person is saying, I haul out the shield and place it in front of me. This shield deflects the remarks right away from me. This Lucite shield helps me separate myself from the stressful situation, and my energy supplies stay intact. I feel no pain, no insult. The shield is impenetrable. No one sees it but me, but anyone separated from me by the shield feels its presence indirectly because of the assured, controlled way I am able to respond to the other person's anger.

Most of us juggle many roles during the day and sometimes the roles and the juggling can cause a stress overload. When this happens to me, and I feel ready to collapse, I draw a circle around my body, much the same way I did in the pain exercise, but instead of driving a wedge into the circle, I go into trance, breathe deeply, focus and remind myself what my primary agenda is. I relax and come out of the trance in a few seconds, altered and refreshed.

A special stress-producing problem that I share with other postchemo patients is fatigue. It comes as a shock that energy levels will rarely return to precancer norms. So one thing I do is try to program time each day for about twenty minutes of meditation or rest and relaxation. The overwhelming urge is to sleep, but that's not always possible. Instead, I meditate and I find at the end of a meditation or hypnotrance, I feel as refreshed as I would after a short nap.

Another technique that enabled me to reduce the stress of nasty remarks or actions was to put the person hurting me on a cloud and float that cloud, mentally, out to the horizon. Out there in the wild blue yonder that person is powerless to harm

115

me. The cloud is not too crowded. The people there are comfortable. I have not hurt them or caused them pain. When I put a person on a cloud in such a lovely imaginary setting there's no guilt involved. I have quite simply neutralized their capacity to hurt me and cause me stress that would deplete my resources.

There are very few people in the world who don't carry around an overload of guilt. But guilt does serve a useful function as far as I am concerned. Guilt acts as a motivator to conscience. But an overabundance can destroy; then it must be dealt with directly and creatively.

During a hypnotherapy session, I fashioned an imaginary "guilt box." Mine was made of black Lucite. It was large enough to accommodate all of the guilts I had from the past or I might accumulate in the future. At any time I desire I can go to the box, reach in, remove a piece of guilt, examine it, deal with it and replace it if I so desire. What a relief! The guilt has a place to sit. I have put into storage a great deal of mental excess baggage, which frees up my thought processes to take off in other creative ways.

As I have mentioned before, fatigue is a big, frightening problem for the postchemo patient, so anything that disturbs a restful night's sleep or interferes with going to sleep must be a cause for concern. I was having a number of problems with sleep, so Dr. Hazelton and I worked in this area. First, I learned how to relax. I found a spot in the middle back region of my head, placed the spot on a pillow and released all weight. Then I slowly put every part of my body to rest. If I was experiencing tension in one particular spot, I visualized myself anesthetizing that area. If I felt achy anywhere, I rubbed the area with Novocain. I don't remember completing the process very often, because I had drifted into sleep.

I was also plagued by recurring dreams and nightmares. The first step in controlling them was remembering them. I often strained myself to no avail the next morning to recall the dream. Dr. Hazelton suggested that I keep a pad beside my bed and when I woke from a dream, write it down. After I recorded the dream or nightmare, I could go to work controlling or working out the problems or fears reflected.

I'd like to share another image technique with you because a lot of women have this annoying problem: hot flashes. One of the by-products of chemotherapy was menopause. It came as a surprise because when I was signing up to be randomized for treatment, no one seemed to mention that the menstrual cycles would end, the reasons that this would be desirable or what theories of estrogen production related to cancer were involved.

Outside of coming to grips with the passage of my biologically productive era, there were small adjustments that helped the situation. I wore clothes, always in layers, for simple on/off relief. I carried a beautiful purse container of perfume to give me a fresh aroma (like in commercials where all women are kissing sweet and scent free) even though I was told repeatedly no odor comes from these sweats. I changed to sleeping in all-cotton lacy nightclothes to help absorb night sweats.

One day as Dr. Hazelton and I were working, I experienced a flash. I assumed I was anxious, since flashes seem to occur more frequently during periods of stress. I mentioned the flash to Dr. Hazelton and she asked if I would like to create a technique to turn flashes around and give them a positive interpretation. Since I am an avid sun-worshiper, she suggested I visualize myself lying on my favorite beach being bathed deeply by the warm rays of the sun. I did as she told me and it worked. I converted the negative to the positive. Now if only I could find a way for a hot flash to tan my skin. But I do find it interesting that when I am cold, I can mentally call up a hot flash to warm me.

Hypnotherapy, or self-hypnosis, is an exciting new area in the frontier of medical knowledge. The techniques are transferable. Smokers use it. Dieters use it. Fear of flying can be overcome in two sessions. Pain can be controlled. To be most effective, sessions should be scheduled just before a trip is planned. A problem is defined, a technique created to deal with the problem. A person is not in continuous hypnotherapy sessions for long periods of time. When the problem is resolved, the patient stops coming until there is a need to handle another situation.

I smile a lot, through my aura of protective lavender. As I face each new day with confidence and vigor, much of it gained through this living, giving, experience of self-activated survival, I am headstrong—through the resources of my faith, the impetus of my hope and optimism, and the remarkable clarity achieved through my work with hypnotherapy.

VOLUNTEERING

I am a firm believer that everyone has an obligation to put back, in some small way, into the community what she or he has received from it. To me, volunteering is simply returning a favor. Neither sex should be exempt from participation. Shared community effort to achieve a common goal is a Judeo-Christian and American tradition. Take a look around. Volunteer efforts are the reason the arts survive in America. Because there are volunteer groups when disaster strikes, some of the horrors are mitigated. Much of the research into the cure of life-threatening diseases is made possible by volunteer efforts to raise funds. Many of the world's hungry and homeless are cared for because people volunteer. Even the health and human services of a nation are made possible, in part, because of volunteer work.

In our family, my mother and father devoted untold hours to volunteer activities. It was a crucial part of their lives. My brother and I always joked that there were really four children in the family, Dan and me, Hadassah and Zionism.

I learned years ago that volunteering can prepare one for career challenges. Before I became a radio broadcaster, I organized a Parade of Torahs and a community rally to show support for Soviet Jewry. I oversaw everything from the printing of programs to the processional arrangements, to parade permits, to celebrity appearances, to prayers for good weather. When three years into my radio career the radio station general manager assigned me the job of organizing the Cleveland Christmas

Parade, I was ready. Five years later, I planned another parade for the opening of the Cleveland Indians baseball team. I had gained my experience in the voluntary sector.

For women, volunteering can be a self-serving activity as well as a self-giving one. For one thing, a woman has only to look around at the needs of the community and then match her interests to those needs. She may not have all the necessary skills to complete the task, but she receives excellent, on-the-job training. Volunteer services give women a chance to experiment in new fields, to try and see if they have undiscovered aptitudes.

Of course, volunteering is also important for those already established in a chosen career. Giving of one's free time, for no pay, to a group or cause one believes in deeply is an indescribably gratifying feeling. One may love one's job, but volunteer work, in addition to a job, has other, possibly deeper satisfactions.

One thing is certain, I couldn't have survived the two years of chemotherapy if I had not had a career I loved. My responsibilities gave me reason to get up and be dressed early every morning. Since the disease defined so much of my life, my career gave me an identity beyond cancer. It was important to me to be able to set professional goals and see them achieved while I was actively fighting cancer. My job also gave me additional financial resources to defray the added expenses I incurred while struggling through chemotherapy.

Nevertheless, during my illness, I found my volunteer work to be the most profoundly satisfying. It kept me involved in life. It eased the pain—physically and emotionally. I would not have survived without it.

Young or old, male or female, volunteering gives purpose and expanded dimension to your life. Aches and pains are temporarily forgotten because you are thinking and doing for someone else.

NETWORKING

Networking is a mutational outgrowth of the "old boy, key to the executive washroom, school tie" syndrome. Women's networking is a variation on a theme. Instead of "If you'll scratch my back, I'll scratch yours," women say, "If we want to progress in different directions, so be it. But because our goals are different doesn't mean we can't help one another. I'll take your recommendation on trust."

The concept is getting together to get ahead. Women ask that favors be extended to someone else trying to make it. Networking among women is an interpersonal, educational, supportive activity. Through this process, women are linked in an ever-widening communications circle. By networking, women build a sense of community across professional and occupational lines that beats the system that isolates women as they move up in male-dominated environments.

In the last few years, a multitude of formal and informal network groups have sprung up all over the country. Some are organized along specific career lines, like women lawyer groups and women in media groups. Some networks have a broader base of appeal, like women in business for themselves or women in nontraditional jobs.

While I was going through chemotherapy, an informal network sprang up among the women in my chemo treatment group. We shared information and gave one another support through the "rip-and-read" method. When any of us read in a magazine or book about a particular abnormality we were experiencing, we would rip out the information, photocopy it generously and take it to a treatment session to share with one another and the doctors.

The source didn't matter. It could have been the *Reader's Digest, Family Circle, Time, Ms., Working Woman*, but if there was an article on women gaining weight during chemo, I clipped it and brought it to the treatment sessions. You can't begin to imagine how many magazines I mutilated at home, in beauty shops, dentists' offices, doctors' offices and waiting rooms of Cleveland during the two years of chemo.

A nagging but unusual side effect confirmed by whatever source was of immeasurable comfort during the years of chemo. To be able to share what I learned with others and to learn from them enhanced our ability to stay in control, to survive. The sharing was also networking at its most basic level.

Networking is a concept I learned about as a result of my activities in the women's movement, but I found the same philosophy worked extraordinarily well when applied to my chemo group or in my relations with other cancer patients. Like volunteering, relating with others in this way provided a special satisfaction and kept me in touch with the world during my illness.

HUMOR

A vital weapon in an arsenal aimed at managing stress is humor. A quick change of pace or a flash of humor can bring instant relief from unbearable pressure, changed body chemistry and the ability to function on a more efficient level.

A woman in our chemo group helped me and everyone else cope with the tremendously stressful situation of the first day of each chemo cycle by sharing a humorous fantasy.

On a Monday, during the second year of treatment, she came running in for her first shot of a new cycle. She said she had stayed away until the last possible minute so that she could be the last patient and not have to endure the long wait. After the extensive preliminaries, she took her seat in the hall with the other patients waiting for their IV injection. As we all complained about the excessive fatigue we were feeling, she interjected, "I think I'm just too tired to have an affair today." She said it to no one in particular, but the remark drew gales of laughter and a few gasps. "Besides," she continued, "if I had an affair, it would have to be with Dr. Sachs, because he is used to one-breasted wonders." All of us were convulsed with laughter. I guess each of us had this thought at one time or another and had sensibly rejected it! We were still delighted and united in the shared comfort of an outrageous fantasy.

Humor helps initiate control, too, when events erode balance and threaten to wrest away dignity. When I feel I might embarrass myself by bursting suddenly into uncontrollable tears, I evoke an image that I know will make me laugh. Humorous images never fail to help me put the problematical and the painful in perspective and regain my composure in public. When anger and pain mount, one gentle nudge from humor restores balance. In a very profound way, humor makes life worth living.

ROOTS
AND RECORDS

I believe that a strong sense of self is derived from some knowledge of our roots. The study of our origins and personal history does provide a way to examine and test centuries-old ingrained patterns and ideas. I think it's important that everyone keep some kind of record of what has gone before. I do this by compiling scrapbooks.

My husband is an expert amateur photographer and provides the material for a fine visual history. I am a saver and a collector of odd items of memorabilia, which augment the picture story. I save the children's report cards, Mother's Day cards, baby teeth, letters of explanation after a misunderstanding, unexpected thank-you messages, invitations.

Together we have created a pictorial and written chronicle in scrapbook form for every year of our life. Our joint effort and our belief in the need to hand down some kind of record to our children is a way, at least, of keeping our intimate relationship current.

Other ways to keep tabs on the past might include keeping a written journal, or the family historian might save letters and arrange them in chronological order. Video and oral taping, especially when done by older members of the family, is also a wonderful way to employ modern technology to preserve family legends, lore—and maybe a few lives. Whatever form the record-keeping takes, it is essential that it be kept.

CELEBRATIONS

There are as many ways to celebrate as there are occasions worth celebrating. What is important is scheduling events to give peaks to the rhythm of life. I couldn't have got through chemotherapy without some joyous occasions to anticipate.

Something as expected as the change of seasons is cause for a party. Something as obscure as Mozart's birthday is excuse enough to plan a celebration. The reason doesn't matter; it's the celebration that's important.

Celebrating and celebrations allow us to create, to be joyous, to work together within the circle of our relationships.

Celebrating and celebrations help us with our volunteer activities by giving us an excuse to party for a cause. We increase our contacts with others by celebrating with our career and volunteer peers, and our friends and family.

How is a life a celebration?

When each moment and fragment is savored and experienced deeply, not rushed over in a headlong drive to cope or suppress, and not submerged in anticipation of a tomorrow. Each day is a treasure with its own gift of hours to be stretched for experiences. Therefore, daily living must be a packed mosaic of celebrations.

Afterword

It's funny how we set up little tests for ourselves. Three years ago I came to Key Biscayne to rest up between chemotherapy treatments, to try and rebuild myself, create some meager reserve of strength for the next onslaught of anticancer drugs.

Down here in Florida, for fitness, all the residents daily walk the beach to the lighthouse at the tip of the key. Three years ago I appeared on the beach dressed in a loose, black cotton strapless sundress with a huge red apple on it, which I somehow thought disguised my swollen shape. I was ready to begin my exercise buildup program. I managed to get from the lounge chair to the beach and then had to rest. After I walked for ten minutes, I had to sit down in the sand to recoup strength enough to be able to get back to my lounge chair.

Today I walked briskly all the way to the lighthouse and back. I touched the rocks beneath the tower with my toe as if to play touch-tag with a new, healthy life. What a victory this represents for me. I would never have believed it possible three years ago, any more than I would have believed it possible that I could be sitting here, completing my story so that I could share my experience with others.

I am in heaven. Surely this must be what it is like. My toes are in the sand, the waves of the Atlantic lick my ankles, my writing pad is propped up on my knees, the sun kisses me on the forehead for inspiration.

This day, on the beach of Key Biscayne, I have completed my dialogue with you. I have shared with you what I think needs to go into a conquering, celebrating headstrong life.

I have taken a risk in sharing my life. I do it because I trust you, the reader. If one personal example or vignette touches you and helps you, it is enough. If one revelation prompts you to say, "This has happened to me, I've felt that, too. I am not alone. I can do that!" it is enough. If by being honest I have helped you look within to find new strength and courage, surely it is enough. Good luck. God Bless . . .

—Rena Blumberg
November 1981

A Few Words
from Experience

CANCER GROUPS

There are many groups around the country that will provide invaluable aid to cancer patients and their families. One of the newest is "I Can Cope," sponsored by the American Cancer Society; another is The Hospice Council of America.

"I Can Cope" conducts eight group sessions led by trained professionals aimed at teaching the patient and family about cancer and how to live with cancer and chemotherapy.

The Hospice Council of America provides at-home care for the dying patient and counseling for the patient and family. A team of physicians, nurses, social worker volunteers and clergy work with the family and patient to ensure that the patient lives comfortably and free of pain until death.

Hospice councils on the local level assist families in arranging around-the-clock home care, educate the public about Hospice, raise funds, train the professional staff and volunteers, and counsel the family during the period of bereavement. For further information, write or call:

National Hospice Organization
1311A Dolley Madison Boulevard
McLean, Virginia 22101
(703) 356-6770

Following is a list of American Cancer Society chapters that can provide information on "I Can Cope" groups and Hospice services in any area of the country.

National Headquarters

American Cancer Society, Inc.
777 Third Avenue
New York, New York 10017

Chartered Divisions of the American Cancer Society, Inc.

Affiliate of the American Cancer
Society
Canal Zone Cancer Committee
Drawer A
Balboa Heights, Canal Zone
00101

Alabama Division, Inc.
2926 Central Avenue
Birmingham, Alabama 35209
(205) 879-2242

Alaska Division, Inc.
1343 G. Street
Anchorage, Alaska 99501
(907) 277-8696

Arizona Division, Inc.
634 West Indian School Road
P.O. Box 33187
Phoenix, Arizona 85067
(602) 264-5861

Arkansas Division, Inc.
5520 West Markham Street
P.O. Box 3822
Little Rock, Arkansas 72203
(501) 664-3480-1-2

California Division, Inc.
1710 Webster Street

Oakland, California 94612
(415) 893-7900

Colorado Division, Inc.
1809 East 18th Avenue
P. O. Box 18268
Denver, Colorado 80218
(303) 321-2464

Connecticut Division, Inc.
Barnes Park South
14 Village Lane
P.O. Box 410
Wallingford, Connecticut 06492
(203) 265-7161

Delaware Division, Inc.
Academy of Medicine Building
1925 Lovering Avenue
Wilmington, Delaware 19806
(302) 654-6267

District of Columbia Division,
Inc.
Universal Building, South
1825 Connecticut Avenue, N.W.
Washington, D.C. 20009
(202) 483-2600

Florida Division, Inc.
1001 South MacDill Avenue

Tampa, Florida 33609
(813) 253-0541

Georgia Division, Inc.
1422 W. Peachtree Street, N.W.
Atlanta, Georgia 30309
(404) 892-0026

Hawaii Division, Inc.
Community Services Center
Building
200 North Vineyard Boulevard
Honolulu, Hawaii 96817
(808) 531-1662-3-4-5

Idaho Division, Inc.
1609 Abbs Street
P.O. Box 5386
Boise, Idaho 83705
(208) 343-4609

Illinois Division, Inc.
37 South Wabash Avenue
Chicago, Illinois 60603
(312) 372-0472

Indiana Division, Inc.
4755 Kingsway Drive, Suite 100
Indianapolis, Indiana 46205
(317) 257-5326

Iowa Division, Inc.
Highway 18 West
P.O. Box 980
Mason City, Iowa 50401
(515) 423-0712

Kansas Division, Inc.
3003 Van Buren Street
Topeka, Kansas 66611
(913) 267-0131

Kentucky Division, Inc.
Medical Arts Building
1169 Eastern Parkway
Louisville, Kentucky 40217
(502) 459-1867

Louisiana Division, Inc.
Masonic Temple Building, Room
810
333 St. Charles Avenue
New Orleans, Louisiana 70130
(504) 523-2029

Maine Division, Inc.
Federal and Green Streets
Brunswick, Maine 04011
(207) 729-3339

Maryland Division, Inc.
200 East Joppa Road
Towson, Maryland 21204
(301) 828-8890

Massachusetts Division, Inc.
247 Commonwealth Avenue
Boston, Massachusetts 02116
(617) 267-2650

Michigan Division, Inc.
1205 East Saginaw Street
Lansing, Michigan 48906
(517) 371-2920

Minnesota Division, Inc.
2750 Park Avenue
Minneapolis, Minnesota 55407
(612) 871-2111

Mississippi Division, Inc.
345 North Mart Plaza
Jackson, Mississippi 39206
(601) 362-8874

Missouri Division, Inc.
715 Jefferson Street
P.O. Box 1066
Jefferson City, Missouri 65101
(314) 636-3195

Montana Division, Inc.
2820 First Avenue South
Billings, Montana 59101
(406) 252-7111

Nebraska Division, Inc.
Overland Wolfe Center
6910 Pacific Street, Suite 210
Omaha, Nebraska 68106
(402) 551-2422

Nevada Division, Inc.
4100 Boulder Highway, Suite A
Las Vegas, Nevada 89121
(702) 454-4242

New Hampshire Division, Inc.
686 Mast Road
Manchester, New Hampshire
03102
(603) 669-3270

New Jersey Division, Inc.
CN2201
North Brunswick, New Jersey
08902
(201) 297-8000

New Mexico Division, Inc.
5800 Lomas Boulevard, N.E.
Albuquerque, New Mexico 87110
(505) 262-1727

New York State Division, Inc.
6725 Lyons Street
P.O. Box 7
East Syracuse, New York 13057
(315) 437-7025

Long Island Division, Inc.
535 Broad Hollow Road,
Route 10
Melville, New York 11747
(516) 420-1111

New York City Division, Inc.
19 West 56th Street
New York, New York 10019
(212) 586-8700

Queens Division, Inc.
111-15 Queens Boulevard
Forest Hills, New York 11375
(212) 263-2224

Westchester Division, Inc.
246 North Central Avenue
Hartsdale, New York 10530
(914) 949-4800

North Carolina Division, Inc.
222 North Person Street
P.O. Box 27624
Raleigh, North Carolina 27611
(919) 834-8463

North Dakota Division, Inc.
Hotel Graver Annex Building
115 Roberts Street
P.O. Box 426
Fargo, North Dakota 58102
(701) 232-1385

Ohio Division, Inc.
453 Lincoln Building
1367 East Sixth Street
Cleveland, Ohio 44114
(216) 771-6700

Oklahoma Division, Inc.
1312 N.W. 24th Street
Oklahoma City, Oklahoma 73106
(405) 525-3515

Oregon Division, Inc.
910 N.E. Union Avenue
Portland, Oregon 97232
(503) 231-5100

Pennsylvania Division, Inc.
Route 422 and Sipe Avenue
P.O. Box 416
Hershey, Pennsylvania 17033
(717) 533-6144

Philadelphia Division, Inc.
21 South 12th Street
Philadelphia, Pennsylvania

19107
(215) 665-2900

Puerto Rico Division, Inc.
(Avenue Domenech 273 Hato
Rey, P.R.)
G.P.O. Box 6004
San Juan, Puerto Rico 00936
(809) 764-2295

Rhode Island Division, Inc.
345 Blackstone Boulevard
Providence, Rhode Island 02906
(401) 831-6970

South Carolina Division, Inc.
2442 Devine Street
Columbia, South Carolina 29205
(803) 256-0245

South Dakota Division, Inc.
1025 North Minnesota Avenue
Hillcrest Plaza
Sioux Falls, South Dakota 57104
(605) 336-0897

Tennessee Division, Inc.
2519 White Avenue
Nashville, Tennessee 37204
(615) 383-1710

Texas Division, Inc.
3834 Spicewood Springs Road
P.O. Box 9863
Austin, Texas 78766
(512) 345-4560

Utah Division, Inc.

610 East South Temple
Salt Lake City, Utah 84102
(801) 322-0431

Vermont Division, Inc.
13 Loomis Street, Drawer C
Montpelier, Vermont 05602
(802) 223-2348

Wyoming Division, Inc.
Indian Hills Center
506 Shoshoni
Cheyenne, Wyoming 82001
(307) 638-3331

Virginia Division, Inc.
3218 West Cary Street
P.O. Box 7288
Richmond, Virginia 23221
(804) 359-0208

Washington Division, Inc.
2120 First Avenue North
Seattle, Washington 98109
(206) 283-1152

West Virginia Division, Inc.
240 Capitol Street, Suite 100
Charleston, West Virginia 25301
(304) 344-3611

Wisconsin Division, Inc.
611 North Sherman Avenue
P.O. Box 1626
Madison, Wisconsin 53701
(608) 249-0487

Milwaukee Division, Inc.
6401 West Capitol Drive
Milwaukee, Wisconsin 53216
(414) 461-1100

VISITING PATIENTS

Through my experience both as a patient and as a visitor, I have made observations about how to converse with a patient, how long to visit, what to bring as gifts. What follows are some tips to make the hospital visit easier for the visitor and more beneficial for the patient.

Most patients need visits as a reminder to them that they haven't been forgotten, but it is always best to call to see if the patient feels up to having visitors. During the phone call find out if the proposed visit is convenient and won't coincide with other friends' visits. Also, if a visit is preplanned, it won't conflict with annoying hospital routine such as the taking of vital signs or when the patient goes for tests.

Visitors worry that a patient might ask them about the severity of the illness or the prognosis. Patients rarely ask these questions of their friends, but if a patient questions the family, the family should respond honestly, or as truthfully as the situation warrants. Patients appreciate honesty and the visitor should listen to the conversation cues the patient gives and participate at the level the patient indicates.

Patients who are sick are usually fatigued, so keep visits short. Remember, you are there to entertain the patient—the patient is too tired to entertain visitors. Keep conversations brief and light, then. Tell them you'll return again soon.

Don't sit on the patient's bed because any unnecessary movement may cause the patient discomfort. Give the patient space. Don't sit too close.

When taking a gift choose something light and easy to handle. The patient can't concentrate for long periods of time or hold anything heavy. Lengthy novels, no matter how engrossing, are out. When giving flowers, less is better. Always provide a container. A small offering can be placed on a windowsill or bedside table.

Don't try to demonstrate the strength of your feelings by what you spend on flowers or other gifts, or the patient feels beholden. Remember, the visit itself is priceless.

SUGGESTED READING

Belsky, Marvin S., M.D., and Gross, Leonard. *How to Choose and Use Your Doctor*. Greenwich, Connecticut: A Fawcett Crest Book, 1975.

Bloomfield, Harold H., M.D.; Cain, Michael Peter; Jaffe, Dennis T. *TM: Discovering Inner Energy and Overcoming Stress*. New York: Delacorte Press, 1975.

Bogin, Meg. *The Path to Pain Control*. Boston: Houghton Mifflin Co., 1982.

Brody, Jane E., with Holleb, Arthur I., M.D. *You Can Fight Cancer and Win*. New York: Quadrangle, The New York Times Book Company, Inc., 1977.

Brody, Jane E. *Jane Brody's Nutrition Book: A Lifetime Guide to Good Eating for Better Health and Weight Control*. New York: W.W. Norton & Co., Inc., 1981.

Brown, Barbara B. *Stress and the Art of Biofeedback*. New York: Harper & Row, Publishers, Inc., 1977.

Cope, Oliver, M.D. *The Breast: Its Problems—Benign and*

Malignant and How to Deal with Them. Boston: Houghton Mifflin Co., 1977.

Corea, Gena. *The Hidden Malpractice: How American Medicine Treats Women as Patients and Professionals*. New York: A Jove/HBJ Book, 1977.

Cousins, Norman. *Anatomy of an Illness as Perceived by the Patient: Reflections on Healing and Regeneration*. New York: W.W. Norton & Co., 1979.

————. *Human Options: An Autobiographical Note-book*. New York: W.W. Norton & Co., Inc. 1981.

Darr, Robert T., and Fritz, William L. *Cancer and Chemotherapy Handbook*. New York: Elsevier, 1980.

Ephron, Nora. *Crazy Salad: Some Things About Women*. New York: Alfred A. Knopf, Inc., 1972.

Fishman, Joan, R.D., M.S., and Anrod, Barbara, under the editorial direction of Jory Graham. *Something's Got to Taste Good: The Cancer Patient's Cookbook*. New York: A Signet Book, New American Library, Times Mirror, 1981.

Ford, Betty. *The Times of My Life*. New York: Harper & Row, Publishers, and the Reader's Digest Association, Inc., 1978.

Fox, Marion Laffey, R.N., and Schnable, Truman G., M.D. *It's Your Body: Know What the Doctor Ordered! Your Complete Guide to Medical Testing*. Maryland: The Charles Press Publishers, 1979.

Fredericks, Carlton, Ph.D. *Breast Cancer: A Nutritional Approach*. New York: Grosset & Dunlap, 1977.

Friedan, Betty. *The Second Stage*. New York: Summit Books, 1981.

Goodfield, June. *The Siege of Cancer*. New York: Random House, 1975.

Graham, Jory. *Understanding the Human Needs of Cancer Patients*. New York: Harcourt Brace Jovanovich, 1982.

Howe, Herbert M. *Do Not Go Gentle*. New York: W.W. Norton & Co., 1981.

Kelly, Orville E. *Make Today Count*. New York: Delacorte Press, 1975.

Kleiman, Carol. *Women's Networks: The Great New Way for Women to Support, Advise and Help Each Other to Get Ahead*. New York: Ballantine, 1980.

Kufrin, Joan. *Uncommon Women*. New York: New Century Publishers, 1981.

Kushner, Rabbi Harold S. *When Bad Things Happen to Good People*. New York: Schocken Books, 1981.

Kushner, Rose. *Why Me? What Every Woman Should Know About Breast Cancer to Save Her Life*. New York: A Signet Book, New American Library, Times Mirror, 1975.

Lear, Martha Weinman. *Heartsounds: The Story of Love and Loss*. New York: Simon & Schuster, 1980.

Lee, Laurel. *Signs of Spring*. New York: A Henry Robbins Book, E.P. Dutton, 1980.

Lerner, Gerda. *A Death of One's Own*. New York: Simon & Schuster, 1978.

Markel, William M., M.D., and Sinon, Virginia B. *The Hospice Concept*. American Cancer Society, Inc., Professional Education Publication, 1978.

May, Rollo. *The Courage to Create*. New York: W.W. Norton & Co., 1975.

Morra, Marion, and Potts, Eve. *Choices: Realistic Alternatives in Cancer Treatment*. New York: Avon Books, 1980.

Pogrebin, Letty Cottin. *Growing Up Free: Raising Your Child in the 80's*. New York: McGraw-Hill Book Co., 1980.

Rollin, Betty. *First, You Cry*. New York: Lippincott, 1976.

Rossi, Ernest L., ed. *The Collected Papers of Milton H. Erickson*. Vol.I, The Nature of Hypnosis and Suggestion
Vol. II, Hypnotic Alteration and Sensory Perceptual and Psychophysical Processes
Vol. III, Hypnotic Investigation and Psychoanalytic Processes
Vol. IV, Innovative Hypnotherapy, New York: Irvington Publishers, 1980.

Ryan, Cornelius, and Ryan, Kathryn Morgan. *A Private Battle*. New York: Simon & Schuster, 1979.

Scarf, Maggie. *Unfinished Business: Pressure Points in the Lives of Women*. New York: Doubleday & Co., Inc., 1980.

Simonton, O. Carl, M.D.; Simonton, Stephanie Matthews; Creighton, James. *Getting Well Again: A Step-by-Step, Self-Help Guide to Overcoming Cancer for Patients and Their Families*. Los Angeles: J.P. Tarcher, Inc., 1978.

Sontag, Susan. *Illness as Metaphor*. New York: Farrar, Straus & Giroux, 1977.

U.S. Department of Health and Human Services, N.I.H. Publication 81-1135. *Chemotherapy and You*. New York, 1980.

Walker, Alice. *You Can't Keep a Good Woman Down*. New York: Harcourt Brace Jovanovich, 1981.

Welch, Mary Scott. *Networking: The Great New Way for Women to Get Ahead*. New York: Harcourt Brace Jovanovich, 1980.

Whelan, Elizabeth, M.D. *Preventing Cancer: What You Can Do to Cut Your Risks by Up to 50%*. New York: W.W. Norton & Co., 1977.

Wiesel, Elie. *Ani Maamin: A Song Lost and Found Again*. New York: Random House, 1973.

Winston, Stephanie. *Getting Organized*. New York: Warner Books, 1978.

Zalon, Jean. *I Am Whole Again: The Case for Breast Reconstruction after Mastectomy*. New York: Random House, 1978.